Musical
Landscapes

The sound of the sea in Fingal's Cave on the Isle of Staffa
echoes through Mendelssohn's *Hebrides* overture.

Musical Landscapes

JOHN BURKE

Foreword by Yehudi Menuhin

With photographs by Ian Pleeth

Webb&Bower
EXETER, ENGLAND

For there is a music wherever there
is a harmony, order or proportion.
Sir Thomas Browne

First published in Great Britain 1983 by
Webb & Bower (Publishers) Limited
9 Colleton Crescent, Exeter, Devon EX2 4BY

Designed by Malcolm Couch

Text Copyright © John Burke 1983
Illustrations Copyright © Ian Pleeth 1983

British Library Cataloguing in Publication Data

Burke, John
  Musical landscapes.
  1. Composers——Homes and haunts——Great Britain
  I. Title
  941   ML87

  ISBN 0-906671-60-4

Typeset in Great Britain by Keyspools Limited, Golborne,
Lancashire

Monochrome and colour origination by
Mandarin Offset International Limited

Printed and bound in Hong Kong by Mandarin Offset
International Limited

For
LUCY HADFIELD
in the hope that
over the years her
music will enrich
our country

Contents

List of Illustrations

Foreword

I am drawn to English music because I love the way it reflects the climate and the vegetation which know no sharp edges, no definitive demarcation, where different hues of green melt into each other and where the line between sea and land is always joined and changing, sometimes gradually, sometimes dramatically. The music is on the whole more fluid, less formal and didactic, than almost any other. On the whole it is a very human music, not given to shattering utterances, to pronouncements of right or wrong, nor to abstract intellectual processes, to human emotion in the abstract but to a single man's experience today as related to a particular place. It is not a music of extremes and confrontation, nor a music of elegant, formal life at court or within the rooms of a private house, but a music that reflects the feelings, thoughts and emotions of particular individuals, finding a sympathetic echo in the hearts of all their compatriots and, if I may add very gratefully, in the heart of one who has come to feel as attached to this people and their land as his far more illustrious predecessors who are described in this book.

The early and high individuality of the British composer was matched by a pervading nostalgia which attached him to his land, to his sea and his climate. Other composers belonged to traditional styles, styles dominating their period, and they were committed to ideas, to structures and to the emotions which relate people to each other rather than to a specific common landscape.

Although the Pastoral Symphony of Beethoven appears to be a vivid portrayal of a summer's day in the Salzkammergut, the storm and the rustic serenity following it take on a universal significance. The storm has been abstracted from its locality and the pastoral scene becomes the nostalgia of all humanity. In the same way, although Vivaldi describes the sounds and the feelings associated with a warm Italian landscape, he does not consider at any moment that his music is depicting a typically Italian landscape.

The British were the great travellers of the eighteenth century and absorbed so much into their own culture, but their land remained their own in a truer and in a more continuous way than any other in our Western world. Even when the British Isles were invaded by northerners and southerners its inhabitants retained their total individuality and their particular and very local rootedness, from which they created the most evolved, democratic, tolerant and hospitable civilization anywhere, perfectly reflected in their music.

This charming book by John Burke gives an account of the many musicians from Europe who enriched British musical life. Perhaps

Handel and Haydn were the two composers who eventually became the most English, though I feel that even they cannot really be set in a specific musical landscape. With Elgar and Vaughan Williams and Delius we are totally within the fold of Englishness. Benjamin Britten could only really compose in Suffolk to the sound of the sea and the marsh birds. Yet he brought to this flat corner of England not only the poetry which reflected the place, but the experience, the sophistication, the styles which ranged across the world he travelled, from America to Japan.

I hope this book will open not only the ears but also the eyes and the imagination of those music-lovers who read it and that they will find the experience a refreshing and liberating one.

Yehudi Menuhin

I
Overture

Music is an innocent luxury, unnecessary,
indeed, to our existence, but a great
improvement and gratification of the
sense of hearing.
Charles Burney

In the summer of 1814 John Constable turned yet again to his beloved Stour valley and made a pencil sketch of boat-builders near Flatford Mill. As summer went on, he sat out of doors at that same spot and worked on a painting of richer scope, capturing the scene and atmosphere for eternity. No-one who has ever been lured into his world of cornfields, river banks and creaking lock gates along the Essex and Suffolk border will ever be entirely released from his spell, or wish to be.

When Turner recorded his vision of Rye looming through mist above the flooded Sussex levels, he caught both the eeriness of the marshes and the glowing defiance of that frequently embattled old town. The communication of painters such as Constable and Turner is direct – the next best thing to being on the spot oneself, and sometimes even better, since in their timeless world the skies will darken no deeper, the grasses will not wither. Through their eyes, our own eyes are taught to focus on a vivid, immediately recognizable world.

Writers work at a distorting remove. In trying to convey scenery and atmosphere through the medium of words they inevitably put up a barrier between their own vision and the reader's ability to interpret that vision. No two people speak quite the same language or in quite the same accent: even the simplest phrase may be mistranslated between one mind and another. Being told, in no matter what magnificent prose, about a green water meadow is a very different thing from being shown an unmistakably green, shimmering water meadow on canvas.

Yet many a poet or novelist has striven to paint word pictures, using words in such order or rhythm as to strike not just echoes but, albeit at several removes, visual memories. Both John Keats and Charles Dickens evoke unforgettable glimpses of the Portsmouth Road, one from a coach and one on foot in the guise of Nicholas Nickleby. Richard Jefferies makes one not merely see but feel the moments spent below a rookery, when flocks dive in headlong descent and then whirl up again with long, gurgling caws, presaging rough weather.

The millstream at Grantchester suggested the second of William Sterndale
Bennett's Three Musical Sketches, Opus 10, in a style similar to that of his
friend Schumann.

Are the words of Robert Louis Stevenson in *Kidnapped* more evocative in
bringing to our senses the sights, sounds and smells of Rannoch Moor and
Balquhidder than, say, the notes of Max Bruch's *Scottish Fantasia* for violin, harp
and orchestra?

Music is surely the most abstract and self-sufficient of the arts. There have been
attempts at abstract painting, prose and poetry; but these defy the very materials
from which they are fashioned. Music has prior claim to being able to exist in
itself, for its own very essence. It needs no plot, no programme, nor even any
obvious geometrical shape, though it has its own disciplines and patterns.
Nevertheless, composers of romantic temperament have been as courageous, or
as foolhardy, as writers: not content with using notes to construct musical forms,
they have tried to paint pictures with them. Even when not deliberately pictorial,
their compositions have aimed to awaken sensations of line, colour, and an
almost physical contact. Their success is often hard to measure: what to one
listener is immediately sympathetic may be meaningless to another.

Given that Thomas Hardy was always in tune with mysterious 'Egdon Heath',
and Gustav Holst was similarly in tune with the author, does Holst's resulting

tone poem give us as sharply identifiable a picture of the scene as paragraphs in *The Return of the Native* do, or as a painting of genius might do? If one of John Ireland's piano pieces had been published simply as an Intermezzo in 1918, would anyone have guessed that it depicted *The Towing Path* in the Thames valley near Pangbourne? Ralph Vaughan Williams's *The Lark Ascending* carries my imagination at once to warm afternoons on my native territory of Romney Marsh, about which the same composer later wrote some delightful film music for *The Loves of Joanna Godden*; but we know it was actually completed in the Cotswolds.

Frederick Delius is usually associated with the lushness and drowsiness of English field and stream. Yet he spent most of his life outside England and often spoke slightingly of his country and countrymen. Without titles it is hard to believe that anyone could detect any great geographical distance between *Brigg Fair*, *Eventyr*, and *Koanga*: the tone of voice is much the same for Lincolnshire, Scandinavia, and North America. Philip Heseltine, Delius's loyal proselytizer, wrote once to his friend to say that when walking into a Cornish sunset at St Merryn he was 'haunted all the while' by the dance from *North Country Sketches*, which seemed to him to express the whole atmosphere of Cornwall. Such a remark can only raise further perplexities about the identification of precise places in musical terms.

This book is an attempt to explore and understand the scenes in which British composers grew up and by which they were inspired; to identify their birthplaces and visit the localities where they were at their most creative. Some moved from those birthplaces but never shook off local influences. Others hated their native regions and shunned them in later life. But this very revolt and the choice of new surroundings are in themselves revealing. If some characters in this story flit erratically in and out of different chapters, that is because in real life they did move from one scene to another, acquiring new strengths and ideas on the way. Some put colourful titles on their compositions, yet denied there was anything crudely programmatic in those pieces. Others used orthodox descriptions on symphonic or chamber pieces which were nevertheless suffused with echoes of landscape and personal joy or grief.

One of the pleasures of working on this book has been that of listening again, often after some years of neglect, to the works of composers who once struck a spark and who prove capable of doing so once more. I am particularly grateful to the BBC for Radio 3, still resisting the attacks of Philistines within and without the Corporation, but would be even happier if they could be persuaded to share these delights with audiences later in the day. During mornings and certain afternoons over a period of many months I have had the excuse and opportunity of hearing nearly every British composer and nearly every work mentioned in these pages. But without the excuse of this specific task, how could I have managed – and how in another profession can anyone manage – to listen at such hours? Come the evening and we are back, with few changes of diet, to the inevitable Beethoven and Tchaikovsky. Critics complain of the neglect of native composers of this century. They can scarcely be other than neglected if potential audiences are never allowed to hear them except at times when most members of those audiences will be out working for their living.

If the following chapters encourage the reader to listen for the first time to something unknown or for the twentieth time to something which may seem to have become out-dated and therefore no longer worth the hearing, then the author will be delighted: gratified not by any smug feeling of 'I told you so', but by the harmonious sharing of resonances which must never be allowed to fade utterly away.

2
Folk and Gentlefolk

Then came the merry masquers in,
And carols roared with blythesome din;
If unmelodious was the song,
It was a hearty note and strong.
Sir Walter Scott

No historical film or television series is complete without its complement of period music. The period may often be hard to define: usually the recipe is a mixture of modal tunes in minuet or gavotte tempo, serving any scene from the days of King Arthur onwards through Elizabethan, Restoration and Regency times. The music, like the characters, is almost invariably decked with furbelows and wimples.

In one respect, however, such film scores have a note of truth. They provide background music – measures for courtly dancing, snatches of bucolic ballad and, at solemn moments, some religious chanting – which is what most performers and listeners throughout medieval times and even during a large part of the Renaissance would have regarded as music's proper function. It was a practical, not a creative art, with the simple duty of accompanying monastic or church services, pageants and receptions, balls and masques. Nobody sat in a reverent hush to taste music as an 'absolute' art form.

As with everything else in the Middle Ages, voices and instruments were first and foremost the handmaidens of the Church. If there were peasant ditties and taproom songs of a cruder nature, few bothered to note them down. Those in monastic orders with an ear for music had plenty of other forms of expression to occupy and delight them: each Mass was an opportunity for praising the Lord with plainchant, whose free rhythms and unison melodies were often more complex than plain; and on the numerous holy days in the calendar there was a great deal of processing to chanted antiphons – two choirs answering each other, or a solo voice alternating with the voices of the congregation.

A royal household offered similar opportunities without the need for monkish seclusion. Henry I employed a group of singers whose main duty was to provide him with music at religious services in whichever residence he was occupying at the time. In subsequent reigns, letters patent confirmed the existence of this Chapel Royal by name. The chapel in the title did not signify a building but, like the German *Kapelle*, a body of singers, attached in this case to the monarch rather

Norham Castle in Northumberland, setting of Walter Scott's *Marmion*,
for which Alexander Mackenzie and Ian Whyte wrote incidental music and
Arthur Sullivan an overture.

than the Church. There were several palaces in and around London where they performed, and when the Court went on tour the musicians went too. Henry VIII took his whole ensemble to the Field of the Cloth of Gold. Early rolls give details of chaplains and singers dignified as 'Gentlemen of the Chapel', with boy choristers and an organist, though at first there was no specific holder of this post and members took it in turn to act as accompanist. Later the organist was, as it were, awarded substantive rank, and among distinguished holders of the position were Tallis, Byrd and Orlando Gibbons.

Honorary appointments to the Chapel within the royal gift were much sought after. One Gentleman in Elizabeth's time had the administration of Greenwich's gardens and orchards bestowed on him. Thomas Tallis and William Byrd were granted the monopoly of music printing and publishing for twenty-one years from 1575 on, and Tallis was able to spend his later years in comfort at Greenwich, where he is buried in St Alfege's church with the enviable epitaph:

> As he did live, so also did he die,
> In mild and quiet Sort.
> (O! happy man)

The monopoly was duly bequeathed to Byrd's pupil, Thomas Morley, for a further twenty-one years which he did not live to complete.

It was Henry VIII who, in ordering the construction of St James's Palace in 1532, established a permanent base for the choir. On the east side of Ambassadors' Court, the Chapel Royal has survived many alterations and additions, its most splendid feature being a richly-painted coffered ceiling attributed to Hans Holbein. A second Chapel Royal, in Marlborough Gate, was designed by Inigo Jones for Henrietta Maria, wife of Charles I, but it was in the earlier building that Charles attended service on the morning before his execution. In more cheerful contrast to this royal death, among royal marriages celebrated here were those of William and Mary, George IV (then Prince of Wales) and his hated Caroline, and George V (then Duke of York) to Princess Mary of Teck.

Today visitors are freely admitted to Ambassadors' Court, and to the Chapel Royal itself for services on Sunday mornings from the second Sunday in October until Palm Sunday, on Christmas Day, and for the choral service on the Feast of the Epiphany when royal gifts of gold, frankincense and myrrh are offered.

A Scottish Chapel Royal was founded in Stirling Castle by Alexander I. Mary, Queen of Scots, shifted it to her palace of Holyrood in Edinburgh, when its functions were housed in Holyrood Abbey church, now a fragmentary ruin as a result of Henry VIII's assault after the Scots had rejected his plan to marry off his son Edward to the young Mary. The body still exists, however, with the duty of providing a dean and six chaplains whenever the sovereign is in residence at Balmoral Castle.

An unadulterated diet of sacred singing was not to the taste of the Tudors or their successors. Wandering minstrels with lighter melodies and secular lyrics were for some time assured of a reasonable welcome at Court, appearing at intervals and hoping always for a summons according to the royal whim. But Henry VIII decided to add another permanent group to his entourage instead of relying on itinerant troubadours. He founded a new organization, the King's Musick, made up of instrumentalists as well as singers – players on the viol, sackbut, flute, rebec and lute. He even included a bagpiper, and was wise enough to add two full-time instrument repairers, but to the chagrin of his subjects he preferred to import foreign musicians, and within a decade had built up the numbers of these talented immigrants to more than fifty.

Even now professional musicians were treated as menials. Patronage for a composer or instrumentalist was indeed, in the derogatory sense of the word, patronizing. For those of musical taste but high birth, the amateur tradition was still the favoured one, though it was no cover-up for royal or noble incompetence.

The ruins of Holyrood Abbey, Edinburgh, home of the Scottish Chapel Royal
from the time of Mary, Queen of Scots.

Kings, queens and princes were brought up to acquit themselves well on instruments and to compose songs and instrumental pieces of a worthy standard. Henry VIII and his daughters were famous for their skill, the king himself writing many songs, supposedly including *Greensleeves*, and adapting others for his own purposes and his own glory. 'Bloody Mary', whatever her other terrible failings, was reputed to be greatly accomplished, 'especially on the lute and *arpichordo*'. Her sister and successor, Elizabeth, established a great reputation as a composer and performer, though she frequently put visiting ambassadors and foreign dignitaries in an awkward position by demanding their opinions on the relative merits of her accomplishments and those of their own monarchs. During tours of the country and at lavish receptions she made great show of her household musicians, but between-whiles cut down their numbers with the parsimony she so often displayed also towards her army and navy – they were much desired when a show of strength was called for, but cast off without a penny once the engagements were over.

Nevertheless, in the consort of the King's Musick, as in the Chapel Royal, there were pickings for the gifted ... or the calculating. Some musicians kept themselves in business by collaborating with their fellows in the Chapel Royal and writing music which required the use of instruments. An instrument maker and repairer who assiduously served both Mary and Elizabeth was granted licences to export ash and secondhand shoes. In James I's time, one Alfonso Lanier had the monopoly of weighing and collecting commission on fodder brought into London, and it was another member of his family, Nicholas Lanier, who became in 1626 the first officially designated Master of the King's Musick to Charles I. By the time of the Victorians this post had ceased to have much administrative importance, and for some time now the appointment has required only that the intendant, nowadays a composer rather than the conductor-cum-impresario of earlier reigns, shall accompany the sovereign on musical occasions and organize music for state occasions such as coronations. In this century the post has been held by Walter Parratt, Edward Elgar, Walford Davies, Arnold Bax and Arthur Bliss. Although it is no longer obligatory for the Master to create pieces for the royal family as his more distant predecessors did, the incumbent at the time of writing, Malcolm Williamson, has produced a delightful *Ode for Queen Elizabeth, the Queen Mother*, first performed privately in Holyrood-house. It is no mere formal, dutiful piece, but an invigorating suite sparkling with melody and good humour, with snatches reminding one of Scottish fiddle tunes, culminating in the lilting dance rhythm of the final movement with a tune full of 'Scotch snaps' or 'Scots catches' – a heavily-accented, short dotted note coming before a longer one, the reverse of the usual practice.

Dissolution of the monastic houses left many musically gifted men with nothing to which they could turn their talents: we can never know how many scholars and singers had to accept whatever menial jobs came to hand. Even if they had renounced their faith and been accepted into the newly reformed churches, they would have found too many changes for their taste: a lot of Catholic music was being systematically torn up, no uniquely Anglican accent had yet established itself, and the dourest among the reformers worked almost as assiduously to ban the gladsome sound of the organ as did later Puritans with their ordinance:

> All Organs, and the Frames or Cases wherein they stand in all
> Churches and or Chappels aforesaid, shall be taken away, and utterly
> defaced, and none hereafter set up in their places.

Whatever deprivation the public might suffer, the royal household remained keen on its pleasures. Charles I was fond of the bass viol, and even when the self-indulgent Stuarts ultimately gave way to austere William III and then the Hanoverians, royal skills did not altogether languish: George I played the viola, and George III was comforted in his spells of derangement by his own ability at the keyboard.

As well as the direct patronage of the Court, favoured musicians might hope under royal warrant for exemption from taxes, urban sentry-go, jury service and other extraneous duties. If they could not aspire to fill any of the few vacant posts at Court, there was always the chance of employment in some noble household, though there seem to have been fewer residents of this kind than popular supposition once estimated. Nor, unlike the royal musician, was the employee necessarily allowed to devote all his time to his chosen occupation. Few of the town or country aristocracy wished to be serenaded all day and every day, and the violinist or harpsichordist was expected to undertake a wide range of everyday tasks. Instrumentalists had to teach the daughters of the family, help with management of the estate, and run errands. Others who served on a part-time basis only were not so much free to seek supplementary opportunities elsewhere as compelled to do so to eke out a living.

But some were lucky. In the dedication of his 1597 set of *English Madrigals*, George Kirbye offered the pieces to the two daughters of Sir Robert Jermyn (one of that family which built Jermyn Street in London) as their 'own ... home bred', since they had been written during his service at Sir Robert's estate of Rushbrooke Hall, a few miles south-east of Bury St Edmunds in Suffolk. After retirement he seems to have been well provided for, living comfortably in Whiting Street, Bury St Edmunds, until his death in 1634. He lies buried in St Mary's church there.

About this same period John Ward, a number of whose madrigals, anthems, and fantasies for viols have survived, served as household musician for Sir Henry Fanshawe at Ware Park in Hertfordshire, and at his town house in Warwick Lane, London.

If an establishment had the wealth to support a corps of instrumentalists rather than just a tutor doubling as keyboard soloist, such players were on call at any hour of the day. There might be a garden party, dancing after dinner, or a masque. On formal occasions their duties were strictly laid down. 'Some Rules and Orders for the Government of the House of an Earl' by an anonymous adviser on domestic etiquette in the time of James I stipulates that 'at great feasts, when the Earl's service is going to the table' they should play fanfares on cornets, sackbuts, shawms and other available wind instruments. During the meal, quieter strains on the viols were recommended. In between such functions the executants would instruct the nobleman's children in the use of viols and keyboard instruments: 'In some houses they are allowed a mess of meat in their chambers, in other houses they eat with the waiters.'

Some mansions provided minstrels' galleries. Most had music rooms set aside for tuition and, if the family was much addicted to music, for chamber recitals. The gallery at Apethorpe, Northamptonshire, has an overmantel carved with King David playing the harp, and the inscription:

> Rare and ever to be wished may sound here
> Instruments which faint spirits and muses cheer
> Composing for the body, soul and ear
> Which sickness sadness and foul spirits fear.

Gilling Castle in North Yorkshire, now the preparatory school for Ampleforth College, opens its hall and great chamber to the public on weekdays between May and September, displaying a frieze of musicians in the great chamber, while the National Trust property of Hardwick Hall, Derbyshire, has a table in its great chamber inlaid with instruments and musical motifs, and Orpheus appears in the overmantel of the withdrawing room.

In the architectural extravagances of Victorian times, medieval trappings were all the rage. Shadwell Park in Norfolk had a monstrosity of a music room which might better have been called a music hall, the size of a large church chancel, with an organ framed in the embrasure of a garish stained-glass rose window. This was later removed by an occupant of less flamboyant tastes. Kelham Hall in Nottinghamshire boasted a two-storey music chamber looked down upon by a colonnaded gallery as in some miniature cathedral nave. In the early part of this century the property was bought by the Society of the Sacred Mission, who added a chapel where one assumes their music is sung today in more restrained surroundings.

One of the greatest English musicians spent a large part of his life lamenting the lack of worthy patronage and a fitting abode in his homeland. John Dowland, who called himself Doleful Dowland, craved a Court appointment, but was kept waiting half a century before obtaining one.

There was for long a tradition that Dowland had been born in Westminster, but Grattan Flood and the great expert on the lutenists and madrigalists, Edmund Fellowes, plumped for Dalkey in County Dublin, where there is a record of John's father having lived and where John was said to have come into the world around Christmas 1562. The surname itself is a variant of the Irish name of Dolan. Although modern authorities, including Diana Poulton, doubt this, no one has yet come up with decisive evidence either way.

It does seem, however, that John was in Ireland when his father died, and at the age of fifteen came to England to serve as a page in Sir Henry Cobham's household. Taken to Paris for three years, he was there converted to Roman

Catholicism. This could hardly have endeared him to Elizabeth I's entourage on his return to England, and his application for appointment as a royal lutenist was turned down. He travelled on the Continent for a further spell, then revisited Dublin, and somewhere along the line he once more became a Protestant. In 1597 he published his *First Book of Songs or Ayres of foure parts with Tableture for the Lute*, shrewdly dedicating it to George Carey, foremost persecutor of Catholics in the realm. Although the pieces were a great national and international success, there was still no Court appointment.

It has been suggested that Dowland's religious vagaries may have been a cover for activities as a spy, paid for out of special royal funds. This would hardly accord with his continuing resentment against lack of royal patronage. In 1598 he went off for nearly eleven years as lutenist to Christian IV of Denmark at Elsinore, where he wrote many of his finest songs. On his return to England there were again hints of involvement in espionage and that he had been paid out of a special fund of James I to pass on secrets about the Danish court.

In spite of his dolefulness, John Dowland seems not to have been in bad circumstances, since on his return he settled in Fetter Lane, which at that time was, according to John Stow, 'on both sides built through with many fair houses'.

A *Pilgrimes Solace* was published in 1612 and, embittered by past neglect, the younger generation's shameless plagiarism of his work, and then by the emergence of a florid Italian vocal style which became fashionable but was alien to him, Dowland entered the service of Lord Howard de Walden. It seems likely that he provided music both at Audley End in Essex – 'a nightingale sitting on a briar in the middle of winter', as he has been described – and at the family's town residence, Suffolk House near Charing Cross.

At last Dowland was appointed one of the six lutenists to Charles I, but this came too late to cheer his inherently melancholy disposition. He composed no more, published no more, and died in London in January 1626. His son Robert was more fortunate, being educated at the expense of a rich patron, Sir Thomas Monson. It is interesting to note that a twentieth-century Lord Howard de Walden was, just before the Second World War, a Vice-President of the League of Audiences, formed during a period of high unemployment to preserve, stimulate and direct cultural recreation into personal, as distinct from mechanized, interpretations of music and drama.

Another composer rumoured to have served as a spy was young Pelham Humfrey, one of the most gifted of the Chapel Royal choristers. In 1664 Charles II sent him off to France, ostensibly to study the methods of Lully, but lavish payment of his expenses was apparently made from the secret espionage fund. One wonders, though, whether Humfrey really had either the time or the

OPPOSITE
In 1634 Henry Lawes, a Gentleman of the Chapel Royal, wrote the music
for Milton's masque, *Comus*, first performed before the Earl of Bridgewater
at Ludlow Castle.

inclination for such activities. His main concern was all for his own musical advancement, if the opinion of Pepys is anything to go by:

> ... an absolute monsieur ... disparages everything, and everybody's skill but his own ... and that Grebus, the Frenchman, the King's Master of the Music, how he understands nothing, nor can he play on any instrument, and so cannot compose ...

In spite of such criticism, Pelham Humfrey's arrogance paid off. He became Master of the Children of the Chapel Royal in 1672, and numbered among his pupils Henry Purcell.

One of the most elusive of sixteenth-century musicians relying on noble or genteel patronage for a living remained little more than a name for about 300 years. In 1925 Peter Warlock paid tribute with the publication of twelve songs in a brochure entitled *Thomas Whythorne, an Unknown Elizabethan Composer*. From it Warlock's friend E. J. Moeran plucked and transformed *Whythorne's Shadow* from a part song into a little orchestral rhapsody for strings, horns, flute, oboe and clarinet, with a melody which sings sweetly and contrapuntally through every part of the ensemble. The shadow in the title derives from the original lyric in which a flatterer is compared to a shadow which will bend and sway according to the desires of the flattered one; but for many years it might well have been thought to represent the wraith of its long-lost composer. All that was known was that in 1571 this gentleman – for so he referred to himself, garnishing his publications with a coat of arms – had issued the first known set of English madrigals, and later a book of duets. The coat of arms suggested a well-to-do dilettante. No more than that could be deduced.

Then, in 1955, the shadow took on flesh, and the landscape through which it had moved took on colour and new dimensions. The manuscript of Whythorne's autobiography turned up and, after scholarly study and editing by James N. Osborn, who also prepared a parallel translation of the author's own weird phonetic spelling, was published by Oxford University Press.

Instead of a leisured amateur we meet a working musician, scraping an existence however and wherever he may. He went to school in Oxford but was forced to leave on the death of the uncle who had been paying his fees. Moving to London, he worked for a while with John Heywood, a musician and versifier, then set himself up as music teacher and performer. From then on his story is a vivid narrative of amorous adventures and escapes. Serving sometimes as music tutor, sometimes as gentleman-in-waiting in various large households, and sometimes both at once, he tells virtuously, but with a suspicion of tongue-in-cheek, of attempts by employers' wives and restless widows to seduce him. He learned to flatter, to dodge, to retreat; wrote arch verses which could be taken as reciprocating love without ever quite committing himself; and on one occasion had to disentangle himself from a relationship threatened by a widow's serving woman who had found some suggestively phrased lines and taken them as referring to herself. He narrowly escaped marriage to a widow who hoped he would care for herself and her two children. Of this Whythorne unchivalrously observed: 'He who weddeth with a widow who hath two children, he shall be cumbered with three thieves.'

After evading both this peril and the attentions of another, younger widow, Whythorne fled to the country to teach a gentleman's children. He is rarely specific about the settings of his various posts, but in this case it seems to have been Weald Hall at South Weald, Essex, near Childerditch where a friend of his was vicar. His employers did not please him too well, but he found time to prepare some of his music for print.

In due course he made his way up to the rank of Master of the Archbishop's Chapel to Doctor Parker, Archbishop of Canterbury, and his name appears among the pall-bearers at Parker's funeral in 1575.

Later research has shown that two years later Whythorne finally found a wife: not one of his over-amorous widows but, according to the marriage licence issued in the parish of St Alphage, Cripplegate, a spinster. One trusts that it was a contented marriage. At any rate nothing more is heard of the man until thirteen years later, when two volumes of his duets were published – the first true duets to appear in England. He survived another six years and was buried in St Mary Abchurch. Just over two months later, his widow remarried. How one would like to know a few more details!

In the autobiography Whythorne makes astute assessments of the different types of musician striving for existence in his day. He discusses organists, ecclesiastical teachers, and those like himself who taught privately in the homes of the well-to-do. And there were the wanderers, those who went with their instruments about the country to towns and villages, hoping to be paid for private performances or at least to raise ready cash in markets, fairs and alehouses; though many were 'of late in this our realm restrained somewhat from their vagabond life'.

In Elizabeth's time the already stringent laws against vagabonds were in fact extended to include itinerant musicians. Any pretty pastoral vision we may have of wandering lutenists charming other pedestrians or the inhabitants of mellow olde-worlde villages, breathing in the sweet air and exuding sweet airs in return, are misleading. Freelances, unless vouched for by noblemen for whom they worked regularly and to whom they were likely to return for a season after touring the provinces, were frowned on by any well-established group they were likely to meet – the closed shop had been invented by the guilds long before our present century. A royal or baronial employee might wander and strum at will, provided he had his authorization documents with him. Others, no matter how talented, performed at their peril: once apprehended, they could expect to be branded, exposed in the pillory for a spell, whipped until bloody, and burned through the ears with a hot iron.

One of the earliest bodies of musicians not directly subsidized by royalty or the nobility was that of the town or city waits – a word traceable back to Nordic roots, meaning a watcher or guard. Every town of any size engaged sentinels to patrol the walls nightly, armed with pipe, horn or drum to mark the hours at

A Norman merchant's house in Norwich became in due course an inn and,
as the Old Music House, home of the city waits, some of whom sailed
with Sir Francis Drake to provide music aboard ship.

which the guard was changed. When danger threatened, an ox-horn sounded the alarm. By the time of the Tudors these watchmen had been supplied with more advanced instruments and, with plenty of time off-shift in which to practise, became not merely timekeepers but serenaders. There were as yet no subsidies from the rates for a Bournemouth Symphony Orchestra or a Northern Sinfonia, but these forerunners did play each night for the entertainment of the townsfolk, provided outdoor fanfares and formal music for visiting dignitaries, and gave public concerts in places stipulated by the city elders. Some families paid for the pleasure of a morning call with soft music.

The figure of a piper marks the town piper's house
in Jedburgh, Roxburghshire.

In Scotland similar functions were undertaken by town pipers, patrolling the streets morning and night with drum and pipe: not the bagpipes, as one might suppose, but a fife. Towards the end of the seventeenth century there was a tendency to discard the fife and rely on drummers alone, on the grounds that the shrilling of a pipe got on the nerves of the urban public and that too many pipers had a somewhat limited repertoire. In his eighteenth-century treatise on *The Rudiments of Music*, Robert Bremner reported:

> I am credibly informed that there is a Piper in a neighbouring Town
> that can only play one Tune; and was you to walk through every
> Corner of that Town, you would hear that Tune, and no other, in the
> Mouth of every Child and Servant there.

Edinburgh followed the English tradition of maintaining a band of town waits, playing about the streets at night and enlivening public functions.

All these groups jealously urged the authorities to outlaw wandering ballad singers and what nowadays we would call buskers. Proud of their municipal or guild livery, local musicians claimed a monopoly of melody in their own neighbourhood. Like modern unions they frequently quarrelled among themselves over various privileges and payments, but they were united against the freelance. In sixteenth-century York, for example, a strict apprenticeship was enjoined under the jurisdiction of the fellowship of local musicians, and there was even the appointment of 'searcher of the waits' to track down any unauthorized stranger presuming to sing or play his fiddle within the city walls. Waits might visit other regions provided they wore distinguishing livery and carried proof of their status. Privately employed consorts might be granted leave of absence to supplement their wages and would be welcome provided they could identify themselves as 'belonging to any baron of this realm or towards any other honourable person of greater degree'. But to emphasize the apartness of the unhappy vagabond, the very name of 'minstrel' was turned into a sneer: 'musician' became the accepted description of those entitled to perform music exclusively with a royal, baronial or civic warrant.

What kind of tunes did town waits and pipers play on their rounds? No libraries of band parts have survived, but there is mention in old records of airs suitable for practice sessions and for performance on cold nights when fingers were none too agile. Probably a number of more technically demanding pieces were adapted from court or manorial consort favourites of the day. And when in doubt, especially in provincial centres, there were always the folk songs which most instrumentalists would know by heart and play by ear. In Scotland the town pipers are said to have relied almost exclusively on folk tunes.

This poses another series of questions. How does one define folk music: does it cease to be folk music if formally arranged according to 'classical' or 'art music' conventions; can we be sure that the supposedly traditional tunes we whistle today bear any close resemblance to the original melodies of the countryside or town streets from which they came; and is the picture of a lost, sweetly simple rural England which so many of them conjure up a true representation or sheer sentimentality?

Cecil Sharp, researcher and founder of the English Folk Dance Society (later amalgamated with the Folk Song Society to form the English Folk Dance and Song Society), used the term 'folk music' to denote 'song which has been created by the common people, in contradistinction to the song, popular or otherwise, which has been composed by the educated'. It seems to me that this definition can lead to some misunderstanding. Many unlettered singers and players who preserved old songs from generation to generation would undoubtedly have contrived variations and refinements as they went, and taught themselves to become more accomplished executants. As for the educated, we surely ought not to assume that once an academically trained musician sets out to capture spontaneous themes in formal notation, the result necessarily loses all validity.

In 1954 the International Folk Music Council wrestled with this problem of definition, and came up with the following:

Folk music is the product of a musical tradition that has evolved
through the process of oral transmission. The factors that shape this
tradition are: (1) continuity which links the present with the past; (2)
variation which springs from the creative impulse of the individual or
the group, and (3) selection by the community, which determines the
form or forms in which the music survives.

   The term can be applied to music that has evolved from
rudimentary beginnings by a community uninfluenced by popular art
and art music, and it can likewise be applied to music which has
originated with an individual composer and has subsequently been
absorbed into the unwritten living tradition of a community.

This austerely stresses the 'unwritten' nature of true folk song and dance, and so
implicitly condemns anyone who tries to imprison, as it were, the spontaneous
nightingale in too rigid a cage. Undoubtedly some gawky phrases of uneven
length and dubious key were too smoothly ironed out by classically trained
interpreters: Granville Bantock's settings of Welsh airs with parlour piano
accompaniment, for instance, pack them too politely into tidy bar lengths with
conventional European cadences in the harmony, dulling characteristic national
inflections. They are a long way removed from the unique blend of freedom and
discipline found in the Welsh *penillion*, when vocal improvisation is set against a
harp continuo. And we have no way of being sure that the current richness of
Welsh choral singing, so much reliant on those conventional harmonies
mentioned above, still carries the faintest echo of the 'singing in parts' mentioned
by Giraldus Cambrensis in his twelfth-century *Itinerarium Cambriae*.

   Yet a great deal of rationalization was done with the best of intentions. We
might have been deprived of many attractive melodies and sudden illuminations
of lost ways of life through old ballads – of work and sport, life and death, loves
and woes – had it not been for the efforts of composers awakened to the untapped
melodic riches of their native lands. In Bohemia and Moravia, Janáček studied
regional speech and song, and incorporated their rhythms and inflections in his
own work. Kodály and, even more assiduously, Bartók, sought out half-
forgotten catches, laments, dirges and dance rhythms of Hungary; and Bartók
pursued trails far into Romania and Slovakia. In Denmark, Carl Nielsen, himself
a vigorous fiddle player at village dances in company with his father, collected
folk songs and endeavoured to match their style when composing songs of his
own so that even at first hearing they should sound as if one had always known
them.

   This criterion would have met with the approval of Ralph Vaughan Williams
when, on 4th December 1903, he first heard 'Bushes and Briars' at Ingrave in
Essex but said he felt he had known it all his life. Gavin Henderson has advanced
the possibility that, while at prep school in Rottingdean, Vaughan Williams may
have heard and been unconsciously influenced by the singing of the Copper
family, generations of whom have preserved old Sussex songs and contributed
many of their own in similar vein; but the composer's own account places his real

awakening at Ingrave. There 'Bushes and Briars' was sung by a retired farm labourer, Mr Pottipher, who when asked about the origins of the melody said: 'If you can get the words, the Almighty sends you a tune.'

In that same year Cecil Sharp, with whom Vaughan Williams was soon to strike up a working friendship, had been equally entranced by 'The Seeds of Love' sung by a Somerset gardener. Gustav Holst was soon drawn into their company when Sharp asked him to arrange and provide accompaniments for a volume of Hampshire songs, and also stimulated his interest in the songs of Somerset. As a result, Holst composed his *Somerset Rhapsody*, beginning with the oboe playing 'It's a rosebud in June' and incorporating other folk tunes such as 'High Germany', 'The Lover's Farewell' and a sheep-shearing song to build up a vision of the countryside giving birth to, yet outlasting, human activities.

The movement developed with such rapidity that mocking reaction was inevitable. Mendelssohn had long ago invited ten thousand devils to take all national music, all 'so-called folk melodies – that is to say, dreadful, vulgar, out-of-tune trash … Scotch bagpipes, Swiss cow-horns, Welsh harps … unspeakable', and now there was to be further condemnation. Ernest Newman derided the folk song movement as 'Solemn wassailing round the village pump'; Constant Lambert said there was nothing to do with a folk song after you had played it once but play it all over again; one critic invented the word 'bogal' to describe the bogus modal character of many melodies; and quite recently a sceptic commented of the collectors that they 'came down like greenfly on rural England'.

Still the quest continued. Gustav Holst's personal interest was passed on to his pupils at St Paul's Girls' School and Morley College when he insisted they should be alert for any songs they might hear on holiday and bring back some record. In eastern Europe, Bartók had been recording more literally on the cylinders of his phonograph. In the British Isles, the Australian-born Percy Grainger was to follow suit.

Grainger found the notation of these unconventional tunes difficult without some actual performance to which he could repeatedly refer back, and realized how important it was to preserve not just the actual notes but the intonations of a regional singer, preferably singing a piece several times over with varying nuances. He never did evolve an entirely satisfactory system of notation, but poured scorn on those less conscientious researchers who did not even try.

Although Grainger was to quarrel with other members of the English Folk Song Society and eventually settle in the United States, his own compositions had profited from his studies. The idiomatic rhythms and intonations had in fact such an influence that it is often hard to tell in his music which is a folk theme setting and which an original piece. His *Mock Morris* of 1910, for example, uses no actual folk tune but all along he had in mind the patterns of the real morris dance. The work pleased him so much that he made versions for several different combinations, the first being for string orchestra.

One tune he revived is unlikely ever again to languish.

Grainger was taken by an *Irish Tune from County Derry* in the Petrie collection of ancient Irish music, and arranged it for various ensembles and solo piano. Charles Villiers Stanford had already made a setting in 1882, and later used the melody again in his *First Irish Rhapsody*; but it was Grainger who truly popularized what came to be better known as *The Londonderry Air*.

He was fond of parody and sly adaptation. *Country Gardens*, a tune also used by other composers, is in fact basically a variation on *The Vicar of Bray*. His *Handel in the Strand* flippantly quotes *The Harmonious Blacksmith*; though it is worth pointing out that in spite of this clog dance's apparent London connotations, the clogs are more likely to be Dutch, since Grainger himself records that he wrote the lively piece out of sheer exuberance upon reaching the Dutch coast after a spell performing inland.

Vaughan Williams did not merely collect folk material and use it instrumentally, as in his suite of English Folk Songs for clarinet and piano, but became so addicted to the Dorian mode (the scale beginning on D and using only the white notes of the piano) and to the use of consecutive triads in the harmonies that even his largest works were conditioned by them: the *Pastoral Symphony*, for instance, reminded Peter Warlock of 'a cow leaning over a gate'.

Yet Warlock himself was reponsible for rediscovering and appreciating many old songs. He managed to keep one foot in the Elizabethan camp, stimulated by poetry of the time and by such of its music as could be revived, and the other foot in good rustic earth. He produced a fine bouncy setting of *Jillian of Bury* from Beaumont and Fletcher's *Knight of the Burning Pestle*, and many versions of Shakespearean lyrics; but also dug out bucolic melodies between Norfolk and Ireland, and set the Lowland Scottish verses of *Johnny wi' the tye* so persuasively that it sounds like an authentic native tune, though melodically and harmonically it is entirely his own creation. But then in all things Peter Warlock was an enthusiast, as hard to confine to one mood as he was to pin down to one region. Here is perhaps a good place to make his acquaintance, though we shall meet him again in differing regions and different chapters of this book, flitting across so many widely-separated stretches of landscape.

He was born Philip Heseltine in the Savoy Hotel, London, in October 1894. His father died when he was two, and at the age of nine the boy was sent to a boarding school at Broadstairs. His interest in music blossomed early, and from Eton – which he hated – he began writing to Frederick Delius, of whose music he was to become an ardent supporter.

At Cefn Bryntalch in Wales, Heseltine tried to study for Civil Service entry, but was continually distracted by thoughts of music. He wrote to Delius of the 'heavenly country' of Wales and said he could 'never tire of such a delicious picture of it' as the one provided by Borrow's *Wild Wales*. Later he spent some time in Gloucestershire, then at Oxford, whose atmosphere he found 'appalling, enervating, and depressing'. At the outbreak of the First World War he was exempted from military service because of a chronic nervous disorder. In 1917 he made an unsatisfactory marriage which soon broke up, causing him to seek solace once more in the countryside. Augustus John, who got to know him later during a spell in Dorset, referred to his 'emotional response to the changing beauties of the landscape'. Staying with D. H. Lawrence near Padstow in Cornwall, Heseltine was delighted by the sinister coastline and the wintry skeletons of trees and hedgerows; and then, in spring, by the gorse burning with a golden radiance.

He was in a mood for settling down and composing, but in the summer of 1917 military medical standards were lowered and he was called for another examination. It was still unlikely that he would be accepted, but the whole idea so enraged him that he went off to Ireland and stayed there for a year. Again the atmosphere worked its magic. He began to study the Celtic languages, and was soon denouncing the popular concept of Irish national melodies: too many of them had been twisted from their original shape into 'folksy' platitudes, and no one without a grasp of the regional language could hope to understand just how melody and speech rhythms should best combine. Heseltine wrote *A Celtic Triad* for small orchestra and a number of songs, including the exhilarating *As Ever I Saw*. Later he was to visit Brittany and seek other echoes in the mystical centre of the Celtic world at Carnac.

As a critic, and joint editor of a musical magazine, *The Sackbut*, with his friend Cecil Gray, he was still Philip Heseltine. But to avoid a clash between the critical and creative sides of his personality (and, it has to be admitted, a clash with fellow musicians who had already felt the lash of his tongue), he adopted the pseudonym of Peter Warlock for his own compositions. Back in Wales, which 'alone holds an enchantment for me stronger than wine or woman, and intimately associated with music', he resolutely settled down to work, refusing to be distracted even by the prospect of visits to his adored Delius.

By 1925 he was on the move again, settling for four years at Eynsford in Kent, where he acquired a large entourage of cats. By now he was building up a persona of eccentricity, pretending to be a rake and drunkard, though his closest friends always denied there was any real substance to this. At Eynsford he wrote the *Capriol Suite* – a very French style of music to emerge from a very Kentish style of village. Here he also put on paper *Yarmouth Fair*, the result of an impulsive car drive to Norfolk in the company of E. J. Moeran and Augustus John.

In a dark mood in London just before Christmas 1930 he felt that his life had been wasted and his work was unappreciated. Later there were also hints of a quarrel with the woman he had been living with. Somewhere around half-past six in the morning of Wednesday 17th December he put his kitten with a dish of food into the area below his flat at 12A Tite Street, Chelsea, closed the doors and windows, and turned on the gas.

It was a sad end for a man whose spirit we prefer to think of singing sweetly in the open countryside or boisterously in his favourite pubs – at Cley and Stalham in Norfolk, in the King William the Fourth at Madron, and the Admiral Duncan in Soho.

Two allied forms of folk song which have been taken up by composers only in comparatively recent times are what might be called the industrial folk song or the ballad of social protest. Such ballads were often the only means by which the peasant or exploited town labourer could voice his feelings, or have them put into

The post-enclosure pattern of Leicestershire fields, about which many rueful
protest ballads were sung, from *The Charnwood Opera* to *The Cottager's
Complaint*, but which in our own time is more happily celebrated by
Michael Tippett's *Shires Suite*, written for the Leicestershire Schools
Symphony Orchestra and local school choirs.

some sort of order for him by literate interpreters: rabble-rousers, some
opponents might say. Some of the older ditties can still re-create a vivid picture of
the country and its customs in the past.

One such was the song of 'The Coney Warren', telling of Charnwood Forest
villagers who met in 1748 to resist landowners' attempts to enclosure their free
pasture and woodland. The tale is a gloomy one:

> The turf is short bitten by rabbits, and now
> No milk can be stroked from the old woman's cow;
> Tom Thresher's poor children look sadly and say
> They must eat water-porridge three times in a day.

There was a fight with warreners in which a man was killed, resulting in the
summoning of two troops of dragoons. After court hearings and much argument,
twenty-six towns and villages were confirmed in their claim to rights of free
common in the forest.

33

The tune to which this saga is set was an old favourite, 'King John and the Abbot of Canterbury', still familiar to us from its use in *The Beggar's Opera*.

Landscapes and seascapes, fields and factories, all added distinctive notes to the country's musical heritage. At Kingsbridge in South Devon the folklorist clergyman Sabine Baring-Gould took down 'words and air, from Roger Huggings, mason, who learned them in 1868 from a man called Kelly in Tavistock' a lament which had survived a century or so, dealing with soldiers leaving for New York to suppress the North American rebels, while wives bade them farewell and 'babes held up their arms with the saddest of cries'. There were dour songs about the early woollen mills; dirges during the cotton famine, and, in our own time, the more sophisticated but still heartfelt condemnations by writers and singers such as Alex Glasgow of the civic authorities' destruction of Newcastle upon Tyne, and the colourful Radio Ballads of Charles Parker, Ewan MacColl and their team.

A study of folk song and protest ballads and broadsheets does make one wonder whether there was ever anything like that idyllic Britain which drawing-room tenors and local choirs try so earnestly to evoke. Before becoming too easily depressed, we must turn to those lovers who have spoken out most convincingly for their country.

When the eccentric Lord Berners came into his title and left the diplomatic service in 1924, he devoted himself to music, with especial success in idiosyncratic ballets. On his estate he paid for the building of Faringdon Folly to alleviate workers' hardship during the worst of the Depression.

3
Land of Lost Content

When people hear good music, it makes
them homesick for something they never
had, and never will have.
                    E. W. Howe

The rivers Avon, Wye and Severn, and the Severn's winding tributaries, embrace many a historic town and historic annual festival. Cheltenham established its Festival of Contemporary Music only six weeks after the end of the Second World War in Europe. Another post-war home for annual celebration of music and the arts has been Bath, whose musical traditions in fact go back further than those of many rivals. From 1705 onwards, a municipal orchestra gave regular concerts in the Pump Room under Beau Nash's patronage, and even thirty years prior to that there had been a 'band of musick' appearing in what is now the Orange Grove.

In 1724 began the long cycle of the Three Choirs Festival, shared in rotation between the cathedrals of Worcester, Gloucester and Hereford. What Cheltenham has endeavoured to be to our contemporaries – though sometimes provoking criticism rather than gratitude – the Three Choirs Festival was to their most illustrious predecessors. In 1890, when it was Worcester's turn, the committee asked an aspiring and still little-recognized local composer, Edward Elgar, for a contribution, and received his *Froissart* overture. At Hereford in 1909 Frederick Delius conducted the first performance of his own *First Dance Rhapsody*, which was generally condemned as 'a shambles' and Delius himself as 'a helplessly bad conductor'. Ralph Vaughan Williams was to present many a new work in these settings, including his *Fantasia on a Theme of Thomas Tallis* at Gloucester in 1910.

Some centuries earlier Hereford Cathedral had numbered among its canons a John Dunstayville, who has been identified, with some reservations, with John Dunstable or Dunstaple, a mathematician, astrologer and composer who won great renown on the Continent. Born about 1390, Dunstable was a major influence on Dufay and shared in that cross-fertilization of musical ideas then common between England, France and the Netherlands. His music was mainly religious, very advanced for its time, but his name has been traditionally associated with one secular song of great beauty, *O rosa bella*, of which there are confusingly a dozen other versions, all anonymous save for one ascribed to John Bellingham, Dunstable's younger contemporary.

Hereford Cathedral, one of the venues of the Three Choirs Festival, where
John Dunstable is reputed to have served as a canon in the fifteenth century
when not travelling abroad in the household of the Duke of Bedford.

One suspects that the misspelling on the gate of Edward Elgar's birthplace
is a sly tribute to one of his most devoted interpreters.

Many of the composers who made their names before the First World War
survived to present further works at Three Choirs Festivals, and in some cases to
see their disciples moving in: Vaughan Williams's younger friend and admirer
Herbert Howells, of Lydney in Gloucestershire, was persuaded by his mentor to
conduct his *Hymnus Paradisi* at Gloucester in 1950 after hiding it away for twelve
years as a purely personal expression of grief at the loss of his only son through
spinal meningitis.

In the middle of the nineteenth century one regular player in the orchestra
during Worcester's contributions had been a William Elgar, piano tuner and
violinist. As a young man, he had been engaged to look after the pianos of the
widowed Queen Adelaide during her years at Witley Court, an honour which
brought other commissions from the local gentry and enabled him to open a
music shop in Worcester. In 1848 he married a girl from the Forest of Dean. After
living over the shop for eight years and producing three children there, they
moved to a cottage at Broadheath, where William and his brother added a small
stable and coach-house which stand to this day. Although a Protestant, William
served as organist at St George's Catholic church in Worcester. His wife attended
services there while he was playing, and in due course was converted to
Catholicism and persuaded William to follow suit. When their fourth child was
born at Broadheath on 2nd June 1857, he was baptized and brought up a
Catholic.

Young Edward Elgar was a moody boy who preferred solitude to the company of his family or other children. From an early age he took piano and violin lessons; but even in that musical household nobody had any inkling that he was to become England's first major composer since the death of Purcell 200 years before.

At school, he recalled many years later, he 'used to gaze from the windows in rapt wonder at the great trees swaying in the wind'. On one occasion he was found squatting by the river bank trying to write down on a bit of music manuscript paper 'what the reeds were singing'. One leading instrumentalist has a memory of Elgar conducting a rehearsal of his First Symphony and imploring the orchestra to play the trio of the second movement 'like something you hear down by the river'. To his friend Sir Sidney Colvin he confided in 1921, when he was sixty-four years of age:

> I am still at heart the dreamy child who used to be found in the reeds
> by Severn side with a sheet of paper trying to fix the sounds and
> longing for something very great. I am still looking for this . . .

Yearning for childhood resonates also through *Dream Children*, the dream interludes in *Falstaff*, and his *Wand of Youth* suite, based on a play devised by himself and his brothers and sisters, in which the crossing of a brook in a woodland glade removes children from the unimaginative reality of their parents' world.

In youth he was fond of riding horses bareback, and later of cycling for untold solitary miles. Even at fifty, in sombre mood, he was grateful for 'my pipe, and a bicycle, and a heavenly country to ride in'. His native county never ceased to enchant him, and when the family had moved back into Worcester itself to run a music shop at 10 High Street, he loved nothing better than interludes on a farm near Broadheath where he could walk, ride and wander. One can understand his being attracted to the 'desolate streams' of Arthur O'Shaughnessy's poem 'The Music Makers', which in 1912 he was to set for contralto, chorus and orchestra.

Edward Elgar left school at fifteen and went to work in a solicitor's office, but he kept up his music, much of which he had taught himself from books and scores in his father's shop. He tried his hand at composition. In 1873 he risked leaving his job, helped his father in the shop and as assistant organist at St George's, and took any casual employment he could get as a violinist in local concerts and recitals until, in 1879, he was appointed conductor to the Worcester Glee Club. He also followed his father into the Three Choirs Festival orchestra.

Success as a composer was a long time coming. Shy and pessimistic by nature, he might have despaired utterly if it had not been for the encouragement of August Jaeger, reader and editor to the London music publishers, Novello. Also

OPPOSITE
Severn reeds, whose sound Elgar sought to capture and which whispered
on in Ivor Gurney's memory.

The British Camp on the Malverns, seen from the Colwall side.

there was the support of his wife, Caroline Alice, whom he had married in 1889 at Brompton Oratory against the wishes of her snobbish relatives and friends.

Alice's belief in Edward was so strong that it led to what might have been a disastrous mistake. The composer threw up all his posts in Worcestershire and moved to London in the hope of persuading publishers to accept his work and of hearing it performed in concert halls and at the popular Crystal Palace, then a great showcase for new works – or, at least, new works by a fortunate few. But soon they had to turn tail, and once again Elgar was reduced to teaching, which he disliked, in Malvern and Worcester.

Several times they made fresh forays to London; and came back. Quite apart from the lack of immediate fame and prosperity, Elgar disliked London and was happy only when looking out upon the Severn, the Teme, and the Malvern Hills. About this time he wrote a little piece which became his first popular success: *Salut d'amour*. Over succeeding years he must have heard it played a hundred times and seen it on hundreds of programmes of salon music, but it brought no financial reward: he had sold it outright to the publishers for two guineas.

In June 1891 the Elgars, with their little daughter Carice who had arrived in the world only a few weeks before the first performance of the *Froissart* overture, moved into Forli, an undistinguished suburban villa still tucked away up a

The house in which Elgar was born
at Broadheath, Worcestershire.

'Loveliest of trees, the cherry . . .' shining in many Housman cyc
piece, Ivor Gurney's *The Cherry Trees*, and Ge

orge Butterworth's tone poem *The Cherry Tree*, a John Ireland piano
's setting of Christina Rossetti's 'Oh fair to see'.

Winfrith Heath, the original 'Egdon Heath'
of Thomas Hardy and Gustav Holst.

gravelly drive in Alexandra Road, Malvern Link. At last he began to make his mark, working under congenial conditions in the benevolent shadow of North Hill. Later he also rented Birchwood Lodge, in woods near Storridge, north-west of the Malverns. It was a rather unimpressive four-square cottage with a stocky porch, tiled roof, and two chimney stacks looking too heavy for the rest of the building; but Elgar loved it from the start and longed always to be back there, able to concentrate without interruption, 'at work in my woodlands'.

It was the British Camp a few miles to the south which provided him with a theme for a large-scale work, helped by some nudging from his mother. Mrs Elgar senior had been staying at Colwall under the westerly slopes of the hills, and was visited there by her son and daughter-in-law. In a letter to one of her daughters she reported a talk she had had with Edward. Making him study the 'lovely old hill' above them, she begged him to write a tale about it. He demurred, but the idea took root.

The British Camp, or Herefordshire Beacon, was an Iron Age hill fort from which could be seen 'one of the goodliest views in England', according to John Evelyn in the seventeenth century. On the slopes towards Ledbury, William Langland had had his vision of Piers Plowman and 'a faire felde ful of folke'. The great earthen ramparts of the fort still dominate that end of the Malvern range, wrinkled like a giant's scowling brow. They had fascinated the soprano Jenny Lind, the 'Swedish Nightingale', whose last home was a house hidden in the trees of Wynd's Point where the main road from Worcester to Ross-on-Wye reaches the summit before its descent into Herefordshire, and who died in 1887 in a bedroom facing the great earthwork. They began to fascinate Elgar, too, and soon his mother was able to write:

> I quite long to have something worked up about it, it's full of interest
> ... And in less than a month he told me *Caractacus* was all cut and
> dried and he had begun work on it.

The inspiration had come at the same time as a commission to provide a large work for the Leeds Choral Union to perform at the Leeds Triennial Festival in 1898. Elgar shut himself happily away at Birchwood to complete what was neither an opera nor a cantata. It fell between two stools but glowed with the elements which were later to fire his masterpieces, and there was, as ever, a sense of the landscape which was not just his own but the land over which distant historic figures had fought in ancient times. Against a musical evocation of morning on the Severn were set the dark resonances of the British Camp by night. Past and present breathe the same air.

Elgar himself conducted the first performance in October 1898, and during that same month and the next worked in a fine creative passion on what must surely be his best-known work, the *Enigma Variations*, introduced the following June at St James's Hall in London under the baton of Hans Richter.

In this set of variations Elgar had put truly living figures into his beloved landscapes. Each movement was graced with the initials or nickname of a cherished friend, and their physical and emotional characteristics were interpreted in music. Elgar saw them against their natural background: the way one walked out of a room, how another strolled across a lawn, how another's dog plunged into a stream. 'Nimrod' was dedicated to his most consistent supporter, Jaeger – German for a hunter, whence the attribution of Nimrod – and it is difficult to believe that any human being was ever offered such a noble, loving tribute in music. The eighth variation seems to have been inspired by an actual house, Sherridge, near Malvern, whose music-loving owners, two sedate sisters, are primly delineated by the composer. The Romanza of Variation 13 has muffled beats meant to suggest the pulsation of a liner's engines, and, together with the quotation from Mendelssohn's *Calm Sea and Prosperous Voyage*, may refer obliquely to what is thought to have been the discreet end of a sentimental interlude in Elgar's life.

The Elgars now moved to another Malvern house, to be found a few doors from the Railway pub on the main road towards Ledbury. Craeg Lea suggests some ancient Welsh name but was really an anagram of the initials of Carice, Edward and Alice added to the surname Elgar. Birchwood Lodge was kept on. It remained Elgar's favourite retreat, though he found other temporary sanctuaries: prickly as he could be, there were many friends eager to offer him comfort and reassurance. A Liverpool businessman invited him for long stays at a house in Betws-y-Coed, North Wales, and here part of *The Apostles* was written. Another wealthy associate, Frank Schuster, had a house on the Thames near Maidenhead, where part of the Violin Concerto was written in a summerhouse-cum-studio on the lawn.

In Germany, the efforts of the conductor Hans Richter made Elgar's a respected name. The English were slower to acknowledge him; unfortunately the first performance of *The Dream of Gerontius* at the Birmingham Festival of 1900, under Richter, was a flop owing to inadequate rehearsal and last-minute illness. It fared better in Germany, but did not appear in its true colours in England for another two years.

In 1904 came a further move, this time to Plas Gwyn in Hereford, with a large garden and orchard above the river. On 5th July a knighthood made the composer Sir Edward Elgar, and a few months later he was offered a chair of music specially created for him at Birmingham University. At the Three Choirs Festival in 1905 he received an honour which at the time probably pleased him more than anything else, and certainly delighted his father: the honorary freedom of Worcester. Later he was to cherish the award of the Order of Merit in 1911 above all others.

Plas Gwyn was the centre for a dangerous hobby. Elgar had developed a keen interest in chemistry, and now fitted up a garden hut which he called 'The Ark', complete with equipment and shelves constructed by himself. Some of these constructions did not long survive: a water-butt exploded, strange smells emanated from the hut – but he was able to patent the Elgar Sulphuretted Hydrogen Apparatus, a title just as resounding and to him perhaps just as satisfying as *The Dream of Gerontius*.

Lady Elgar died in April 1920. The prop thus knocked away could never be replaced. The widower wrote: 'There is no work left for me to do: my active creative period began under the most tender care and it ended with that care.'

He had previous commitments to fulfil in London and elsewhere, and mechanically went through with them. He was back in Hereford for the Three Choirs Festival in 1921, but soon after his daughter's marriage he felt the tug of his home county once more, and moved into Napleton Grange, about five miles from Worcester. Still he was restless, leaving one house when the lease ran out and finding another, always in the same region, until at last he settled in Marl Bank on Rainbow Hill, Worcester, with views of the city and the countryside beyond. There were old friends to talk to; concerts to conduct if he felt in the mood; hours to spend contemplating his favourite view, that from the window of the cathedral library down-river towards the hills; and a few compositions to work on, in spite of his own conviction that the spark within him had died.

In the garden of Marl Bank was once a piece of the stone parapet from old Worcester bridge, replaced and opened by the Prince of Wales in 1932. The parapet was later removed to Broadheath village, and the house has been replaced by a block of flats called Elgar Court.

During 1933 Elgar conducted with the young Yehudi Menuhin as soloist, and appeared at that year's Three Choirs Festival in Hereford, but it was becoming clear that he was seriously ill. From his own house during the last days, and in great pain after an operation which had failed to cure a malignant tumour, he supervised a recording session in London. Lawrance Collingwood was conducting the Triumphal March and the Woodland Interlude from *Caractacus*, and by use of a telephone landline it was possible for the dying composer to set his seal on the last of his own works he was to hear, and to approve of the playback.

His own countryside was a solace, as it had always been. He dreamed and talked of the river Teme – 'surely the most beautiful river that ever was' – and when in acute pain and unable to sleep, seemed to wander in memory along its banks, declaring that he wished to have his ashes scattered on its waters. When he died on 23rd February 1934, however, he was buried beside his wife in St Wulstan's churchyard, Little Malvern, where they were joined in 1970 by their daughter Carice. His birthplace at Broadheath was bought by Worcester corporation and fitted out as a miniature museum with personal mementoes brought in by friends. At the opening of the Three Choirs Festival in 1935 a window was dedicated to his memory in Worcester Cathedral.

There is a bronze bust in Priory Park, Malvern, and on the way along Jubilee Drive to the British Camp the visitor will be shown his favourite place of meditation on the western rim of the Malverns. A more impressive bronze, this time a life-size statue by Kenneth Potts, a local sculptor, was unveiled by Prince Charles on 2nd June 1981. Behind it, a small blue plaque above the windows of a department store marks the position of the family shop in High Street which was pulled down during the construction of the modern shopping precinct.

At the unveiling ceremony of the statue, two elderly people were given privileged places. One was Mrs Frances Mountford, who had been Elgar's housekeeper for several years at his last home, Marl Bank, and whose late husband had been his chauffeur and valet. The other was Harold Tolley of Alfrick, who had worked for the County Garage near Napleton Grange when Elgar lived there, and was often engaged to drive the composer around some of his favourite beauty spots – Birtsmorton, Castlemorton, and the Malvern region.

Rodney Baldwyn, organist at Pershore Abbey, has a strange tale to tell of two impressions he had in 1976 of Elgar's presence at a certain spot along a lane between Drakes Broughton and Wadborough. It was only some while later that he read Basil Maine's book about Elgar, in which his liking for that stretch of road was mentioned, together with his hope that it was here he 'intended to return' if it were at all possible, 'moving leisurely along those green ways'.

It seems odd that, with such a melancholy and introspective disposition, Elgar should never have tried his hand at setting the poems of another gifted melancholic from his own county. Perhaps A. E. Housman's pagan pessimism was distasteful to Elgar's Roman Catholic piety; or perhaps he felt that the poet, by adopting for his most famous sequence of verses the name of another county, had somehow denied his Fockbury birthplace. But if ever there were a germinative influence in this region, it was the dour Housman and his little volume *A Shropshire Lad*. As scholar and critic he was austere and misanthropic, the terror of Cambridge students. As a lyricist he created a wistful, dying music which he felt needed no further ornamentation. He would not have agreed with the medieval troubadour's declaration that 'a verse without music is a mill without water'. At a Trinity College dinner, Housman scathingly denounced settings by Butterworth and Vaughan Williams of his poems and fiercely ordered his neighbour, Herbert Howells, never to attempt anything similar. Howells had in fact recently tried his hand at just such settings but now, in great trepidation, he destroyed them.

Of those who were to add the most distinguished music to *A Shropshire Lad*, none came from Shropshire, any more than Housman had done. George Butterworth was born in London, Arthur Somervell at Windermere, Ralph Vaughan Williams and Ivor Gurney in Gloucestershire, and John Ireland in Cheshire.

One of the first to make a selection was George Butterworth. Born in 1885, he showed precocious musical talent while still at Eton, but for a while seemed likely to turn out little more than a dilettante. After leaving Oxford he was for a while assistant music critic on *The Times*, went on to become music master at Radley, then left in 1910 to study more seriously at the Royal College of Music. He had already been attracted by the folk song and dance movement, collected a number of *Country Dance Tunes* and *Folk-songs from Sussex*, and wrote a little orchestral tone poem still frequently played, *The Banks of Green Willow*. This idyll appeared in 1914, springing from fragments of folk tune linked and sported with in the most easy-going way, and most richly scored in a short section for four cellos.

When it came to setting Housman's words for voice and piano, Butterworth chose six poems for his cycle *A Shropshire Lad* and another five for *Bredon Hill*.

Bredon Hill, where in summertime the bells sound so clear.

There is also *A Shropshire Lad Rhapsody*, written not as an overture but rather as an orchestral epilogue, using some of the material from the first song cycle. Butterworth's style is more direct and, on the face of it, much simpler than that of some who followed him in adapting the same material. But the simplicity is that of strength and confidence; it would be hard to find two more beautiful tunes than those he used for 'Loveliest of trees, the cherry now' and 'The lads in their hundreds'. In a way, this latter is almost too lilting and attractive – after all, it implies the fate of young men coming into Ludlow to the fair and going on to some battlefield where they will 'die in their glory and never be old'. Its attitude is more that of the romantic Rupert Brooke than Wilfred Owen. Utterly different was Ivor Gurney's interpretation of the same poem – dark, urgent, with an insistent martial rhythm, in much the same mood as his 'On the idle hill of summer' through which beats the menacing 'steady drummer'. Both these composers suffered fates poignantly apposite to their music: Butterworth was killed on the Somme in 1916; Gurney, wounded and then gassed at Passchendaele, suffered delayed shell-shock and soon after the First World War was committed to an asylum.

Born in Queen Street, Gloucester, in August 1890, Ivor Gurney had become a choirboy at the cathedral thanks to the encouragement of the curate of his parish church, Alfred Cheesman. Loving the countryside and caught up in his own poetical and musical thoughts, the boy was another solitary like Elgar and was known to his school friends as 'Batty Gurney' – a sad omen of what was to come after the war years. He had a particular affection for a group of Gloucestershire villages and certain hilltops. His close friend Herbert Howells tells of one radiant morning when the cathedral's east window glowed with such overwhelming splendour that young Ivor cried out, 'God, I must go to Framilode', went off without more ado, and did not come back for three days. Howells's early Piano Quartet is dedicated to 'the hill at Chosen and Ivor Gurney who knows it' – 'Chosen' being Churchdown Hill between Cheltenham and Gloucester, from which in varying weathers one catches pale, dark or sparkling glimpses of the Malverns.

At the outbreak of war in 1914 Gurney was rejected for military service because of defective eyesight. In February 1915 he tried again and this time was accepted into the 2nd/5th Gloucesters. In the trenches he wrote poetry and even songs, one of them a setting of a poem by his friend F. W. Harvey about Gloucestershire's fields and rivers; and at Caulaincourt in March 1917 one short, heartbreaking setting of his own verses, imploring

> Do not forget me quite,
> O Severn meadows.

This same brief poem was later to be set even more beautifully by Gerald Finzi, who worked as hard to achieve recognition for Gurney as he ever did on his own behalf.

After the war the results of his wound, gassing and shell-shock contributed to what Gurney's acquaintances considered had always been an inherent instability.

The view towards Cheltenham from one of Ivor Gurney's favourite vantage
points, Cleeve Hill in Gloucestershire.

He continued writing poetry and music, but unfortunately he also wrote
rambling letters to friends and relatives, and when discharged from the army had
a habit of disappearing and wandering round his beloved hamlets, returning with
weird and inconsistent tales of his doings. Trying to cling to sanity, in letters he
recited litanies of his particular joys: Cleeve, Crickley, Cranham, Lackhampton,
Shurdington, Brockworth ... and always that dominating cathedral 'standing
out grey in the distance'. Friends took him on long walks in the Black Mountains
and on holiday to Cornwall, where a risky rock climb near Gurnard's Head
produced spontaneously a setting of *Desire in Spring* from a poem by Francis
Ledwidge.

He tried studying composition under Ralph Vaughan Williams at the Royal
College of Music; found lodgings in Earls Court; then moved out to High
Wycombe to supplement his inadequate army pension as organist at St Michael's
church. Still he kept writing. In all he was to compose 250 songs, of which around
ninety are known or ought to be known: the rest, according to his biographer
Michael Hurd, are 'of curiosity value only'.

Through 1920 and 1921 Herbert Howells grew more and more worried about
his friend, and with good reason. Gurney wandered between London and
Gloucester, often sleeping rough, impulsively disappearing into the countryside.
He found a cottage at Dryhill near Witcombe; then decided it wouldn't do, but
continued to spend time at Dryhill Farm. He began to have hallucinations and
was sure his mind was being deliberately attacked by electrical waves. In October

1922, friends subscribed to find him a place in a private asylum on the edge of Gloucester. Visitors disturbed rather than comforted him, and in the end he had to be transferred to the City of London Mental Hospital at Dartford. Here he wrote some good poems and some incoherent ones, eventually sinking into utter insanity but lingering on until Boxing Day 1937. He lies buried in Twigworth churchyard just outside Gloucester, where his mentor Alfred Cheesman had become vicar in 1912. Of his two Housman song cycles, *Ludlow and Teme* was published in 1923; by the time the second set, *The Western Playland*, was issued in 1926, he had been shut away for four years.

Arthur Somervell, born at Windermere in 1863, had led a more conventional academic existence as professor at the RCM, inspector of music in schools, and later the official inspector of music to the Board of Education. But he, too, had his rural yearnings. He edited British folk songs in *Songs of the Four Nations* and he, too, succumbed to the lure of Housman by producing his own selection from *A Shropshire Lad*.

In 1921 John Ireland took a rueful line from one of the poems as title for a cycle of seven songs: *The Land of Lost Content*. Himself an introspective pessimist, Ireland had much in common with the poet and admired his ability 'to say so much in such a condensed way'. He also wrote a couple of separate songs, *Hawthorn Time* and *The Heart's Desire*, on Housman themes, and, like Butterworth, perhaps inspired by Housman or perhaps just by an instant of visual joy, wrote a piece called simply *The Cherry Tree* – in Ireland's case, for solo piano.

E. J. Moeran, who studied with Ireland after First World War service, wrote a Housman cycle called *Ludlow Town*.

But the musical interpretation which most people today associate with Housman's poetry, in spite of the poet's own disparagement, is the 1909 cycle *On Wenlock Edge* by Ralph Vaughan Williams, a close friend of Butterworth. His settings are more pictorial and programmatic than those of other composers in the same field; the whole cycle has an inner unity which the rival sets of individual songs never quite achieve, and the almost symphonic strength of piano and string quartet accompaniment proved easy to expand later into a version for string orchestra.

From January 1908 Vaughan Williams had spent some months in Paris studying with Ravel, and his subsequent work on the Housman verses displays an impressionistic technique which must owe something to that French contact. In the opening song the woods on Wenlock Edge are troubled by a flurry of urgent trills and tremoloes, with stormy rustling in the strings and agitated triplets in the piano part. Bells peal through a haze on Bredon Hill which is almost tangible. One vibrant chord of the thirteenth recurs and echoes so hauntingly in our memories that it has come to be referred to simply as 'the Wenlock Edge chord', shimmering on the eternally restless horizon. The melodies throughout are original, yet a folk song element sings to itself somewhere not too far away and comes closer in the Dorian mode of 'Oh, when I was in love with you'. The final song, 'In valleys of springs of rivers', is headed merely 'Clun' by the composer, who sketched it out some years earlier as a piece in its own right; but it provides a fitting conclusion, with its final drift from the minor into a tranquil, all-absolving major.

One particular echo nags at me whenever I hear the Butterworth or Vaughan Williams interpretation of 'Is my team ploughing?' Ivor Gurney also used this poem, but with less impact than the other two. At the end both Butterworth and Vaughan Williams leap the same interval to achieve the eerie unease of the living man's answer to the questioning ghost:

> I cheer a dead man's sweetheart,
> Never ask me whose.

Was the similarity a deliberate tribute from one friend to another, or simply an unconscious borrowing? Certainly they were very close. It was Butterworth who urged Vaughan Williams on to complete his *London Symphony*, and to Butterworth it is dedicated: a memorial to the fellow composer who was just beginning to fulfil his promise when war silenced him forever.

Ralph Vaughan Williams was born on 12th October 1872 in the vicarage at Down Ampney in Gloucestershire, the youngest of three children. Their father had married a daughter of Josiah Wedgwood III in the same year as his appointment as vicar to Christ Church in that village, and all the children were baptized here. The father died three years after Ralph's birth and is buried in Down Ampney churchyard beside the south transept, in which there is a memorial window with a resurrection scene. Between 1972 and 1979 an appeal for funds in memory of Ralph Vaughan Williams himself made possible the restoration and extension of the church organ.

The widow took her little girl and two boys back to her old home at Leith Hill Place in Surrey, where her father lived on until 1890 and her sister Sophie proved an affectionate companion to young Ralph, encouraging his obvious interest in music. An organ was installed for him in the house; he was taught the violin; in the year of his grandfather's death he went to the RCM for the first of two periods of study, also studying for a short time with Bruch in Berlin and, as we have seen, with Ravel in Paris.

Wherever his later work took him, he never lost his affection for Leith Hill Place, commanding as it did a magnificent view across the Surrey border into Sussex. When studying at the Royal College he would often on a fine weekend walk all the way back, making the most of the scenery and the fresh air. After joining the Folk Song Society he readily responded to Cecil Sharp's injunction not to sit around discussing the subject but to get out into the open and hunt for the real thing. As a lover of the outdoors, and in conscious search of an intrinsically English mode of musical expression to replace what he called the 'off-scourings' of established European classics, Vaughan Williams found such field-work a rewarding rather than arduous task. He reaped a gratifying harvest from the Sussex Weald near his home, and paid further visits to Essex and on into the Fens and Norfolk.

At about this same time he had been commissioned to add a number of tunes to

53

On Wenlock Edge the wood's in trouble.

At the time of Ralph Vaughan Williams's birth, his father was vicar
of Down Ampney, commemorated in the hymn tune of that name.

the inadequately revised *Hymns Ancient and Modern*, which had not come up to the standard expected of it. After intensive research Vaughan Williams found himself with enough material for a quite separate volume which became *The English Hymnal*. He dug out verses and tunes from other parts of the world and from all over his own country, and inevitably incorporated a number of folk tunes: *Monk's Gate*, for example, is called after the hamlet a few miles south of Horsham where he first heard it. He also added some melodies of his own, including a tribute to his birthplace in *Down Ampney*, and later was to contribute in similar vein to the *Oxford Book of Carols*.

From this collecting of hymns came the spark for one of his own most successful orchestral works. Number 92 in *The English Hymnal* is a modal tune by Thomas Tallis on which Vaughan Williams constructed a Fantasia, first performed in 1910, which in every bar may be truly said to 'speak for England'.

In 1905 his sister and Lady Farrer had suggested starting an annual festival, largely for the benefit of local choirs. Over the years Vaughan Williams contributed so much to this Leith Hill Festival that it became almost as firmly associated with his name as Aldeburgh in our own time has been associated with Benjamin Britten.

In 1914 Vaughan Williams wrote *The Lark Ascending*, but the outbreak of war delayed its performance. He served in Macedonia and France, and on return to England became Professor of Composition at the RCM. Not until 1921 did there come the first performance of that orchestral piece whose score he had prefaced with a quotation from George Meredith:

> He rises and begins to round,
> He drops the silver chain of sound,
> Of many links without a break,
> In chirrup, whistle, slur and shake.

Final touches had been put to the work in the Cotswolds, and one writer has commented that the whole effect is of a lark flying above a landscape as varied as that glowing region. But often the lark is hovering and not moving on: time stands still, the trilling bird hangs high above the world in a pure light, magically sustained in infinity, while all murmurings below are suppressed to the lightest, wariest breathing. Elizabeth Barrett Browning puts it more succinctly than Meredith:

> The music soars within the little lark,
> And the lark soars.

In 1922 came the *Pastoral Symphony*. Many of the Vaughan Williams symphonies are remembered, and were referred to by the composer, by titles rather than numbers; and in many ways they have the character of symphonic suites rather than academically disciplined symphonies. The use of a soprano or tenor soloist in the *Pastoral* gives us people in a landscape, not just abstract vocal lines. Tunes grow out of one another like plants putting out shoots and intertwining, and the mood is one of rural meditation, never of blunt statement.

In this and subsequent works, the composer's reliance on modal themes and the eccentric rhythms of folk song and dance was inevitably in conflict with any attempt to shape the material into conventional patterns; in this conflict his love for English characteristics won every time.

The critic Ernest Newman's response to these elements taken in conjunction with a vision of English fields in summertime and the works of his favourite English poets from Chaucer onwards was that 'when Vaughan Williams joins the company with certain compositions of his I find that this music is English to its very marrow'.

Herbert Howells, twenty years Vaughan Williams's junior, felt much the same and never forgot first hearing the *Fantasia on a Theme by Thomas Tallis* in Gloucester cathedral. The night of that experience, he and Ivor Gurney roamed the Gloucester streets quite unable to sleep; but only after the First World War did Howells and Vaughan Williams become really close friends – an 'intuitive affinity' was the way Howells described their relationship.

He studied under the dogmatic Stanford at the RCM and, in spite of differences between them, was given a useful start when his professor submitted his Piano Quartet for sponsorship by the Carnegie Trust. Howells had the same affection for his home county shown by several gifted contemporaries, and among his most fluent works is the string quartet, his third, entitled *In Gloucestershire*. Its first movement delineates the river Severn and the summery Cotswolds; the second is spiky, sprightly and thrusting; the third suggests a deep but never mawkish personal grief similar to that which suffuses the *Hymnus Paradisi*, though the tragedy which prompted that work still lay in the future; and in the fourth we are dancing to tunes suggestive of the Welsh borderlands.

It may come as a disappointment for those of romantic temperament, though, to hear that Howells's charming little choral piece *A Spotless Rose* was, according to his own wry testimony, composed while he was idly watching shunting on a railway siding in Gloucester.

On the far side of what we loosely describe as the Midlands, east of those mystical western marches, we find a remarkable richness of music emerging from the town of Northampton.

Edmund Rubbra, born in 1901, left school at fourteen and got a job as correspondence clerk in the London and North Western Railway Permanent Way Department. Three years later he came across the music of Cyril Scott and was so entranced that he raised as much money as he could scrape together to put on a chamber recital. Scott himself got to hear of this and, intrigued, offered to take the young man on as a pupil; so once a fortnight Rubbra took advantage of one of his perks as a railway employee and travelled to and from London on a half-price ticket. His first work of any substance, a tone poem for piano and orchestra, was given an unfortunate title which he never ceased to regret: *Nature's Call*. After that early period of admiration, Cyril Scott's influence seems to have waned. Rubbra's symphonies and large choral works are all not only traditional but, in the view of some serialists and 12-tone row addicts, downright reactionary. Steeped in the joys of Tudor polyphony, he has never shown any sign

Lydney, birthplace and for long the home of Herbert Howells.

of compromise, though he has occasionally reacted to certain catalysts: his stylish *Improvisations on virginal pieces by Giles Farnaby* display his Elizabethan bent, but at the same time show more than a touch of Vaughan Williams.

Reminiscing on the radio programme *Desert Island Discs* to mark his eightieth birthday in 1981, Rubbra told of one hot summer evening far back in his youth when he had walked some way from Northampton and leaned on a stile to look back at the town through the haze. Distant bells sounded through the still air. Rubbra never forgot their sound or the setting, and repeatedly uses bell sounds and strange carillons in his music.

Without descending to the cheap chimes of bells across the meadow or tinkling in a monastery garden, rung by Albert Ketèlbey, that most popular of late nineteenth-century composers in England (far more frequently performed than Beethoven), we might lend an ear to the effect of bells on other composers: bells sounding so clear on Bredon; Samuel Wesley and Holsworthy church bells; the blind French organist Louis Vierne of Notre-Dame who in 1925 played in St Mary's church at Hinckley in Leicestershire and wrote a piece called *Les Cloches de Hinckley*, as well as *Le Carillon de Westminster*; and the modern Jonathan Harvey, so fascinated by the resonances of a Winchester cathedral bell that he works on electronic analysis and recording of its harmonics.

Other Northampton composers include William Alwyn and the prolific Malcolm Arnold, whose interests spread from Scottish dances to Cornish dances, from brass bands (he was a trumpeter in the London Philharmonic Orchestra) to the most tuneful guitar and flute concertos. And among younger composers of our own time, Trevor Hold has used folk tunes in *The Lilford Owl* in tribute to the work of Grieg and Percy Grainger.

On the subject of folk songs, one does wonder at the ubiquity of the oboe. Pastoral pictures of shepherd lads whiling away the time usually suggest that they are playing a flute or pipe of some kind. Yet to evoke the English atmosphere, every composer of any significance has tended to rely on the oboe's reedy tone. Elgar's *Soliloquy for oboe and orchestra* is as rural as anything he ever wrote. Vaughan Williams's symphonic impression *In the Fen Country* uses one of his own derivative melodies rather than an original folk tune, but the plaintive oboe gives it a sly suggestion of authenticity, starting the piece and insinuating itself back into it from time to time. His Oboe Concerto is less a concerto than a rhapsody on intrinsically pastoral themes. In Frank Bridge's tone poem, *Summer*, we are drawn over a tremor of strings by an oboe theme floating and looping like a butterfly above the grass. Moeran's *Lonely Waters* offers an introductory fragment of genuine Norfolk folk song on the oboe, which returns after a quiet but intense dialogue between strings and woodwind. George Butterworth's *Two English Idylls* both begin on the oboe; and it comes as quite a shock to turn to that other Butterworth idyll, *The Banks of Green Willow*, and find oneself being led in by a clarinet.

Vaughan Williams, admittedly, did use clarinet and piano for his *Six Studies in English Folk Song*. And Gerald Finzi's *Five Bagatelles* for clarinet and piano, though more adventurous and individualistic, still have a rural ambience – frisky little songs without words, rippling away on the fringe of an easy-going *fête champêtre*.

Gerald Finzi belonged for a while in the Gloucestershire scene. Born in London in 1901, he studied music with Ernest Farrar between 1914 and 1916, and was deeply shocked when Farrar was killed only a few days after going to France. Much of his life seems to have been shadowed by loss: his father died when he was only eight, and his three elder brothers all predeceased him. In 1922 he shut himself away at Painswick in Gloucestershire in order to work.

By 1925 he was back in London, trying to make his mark, and between 1930 and 1933 was Professor of Composition at the Royal Academy of Music. Two years after his marriage in 1933 he retired again to the countryside, continuing to work in his own reflective way at Aldbourne in Wiltshire. In 1937 the Finzis crossed the border into Hampshire, found a hillside site at Ashmansworth, and built a house designed specially to suit his working methods. Under the porch Finzi buried a copy of his favourite among his own songs, a setting of James Elroy Flecker's 'To a poet a thousand years hence'.

In spite of his somewhat withdrawn nature, Finzi was generous with his time in the cause of others. He battled not merely against public indifference but against the reservations and non-cooperation of friends and relatives when trying to

The house in which Gerald Finzi worked at Ashmansworth in Hampshire.

make Ivor Gurney's work better known; and he was a constant source of strength to his friend Robin Milford, though Milford did lament that Finzi's 'own settings of Hardy are at once my delight and my despair'.

During the Second World War, Finzi worked in London for the Ministry of War Transport, but continued to keep an eye on the semi-amateur group he had formed, the Newbury String Players. The *Five Bagatelles* for clarinet and piano were composed during this period and first performed at one of the wartime National Gallery concerts.

In 1951 he discovered that he was suffering from leukemia. Weakened by this affliction, he was an easy prey when he came into contact with a case of chickenpox during the 1956 Gloucester Festival, and died after contracting shingles.

Finzi's fastidious setting of poetry rarely relied on conventional musical phrase lengths. The words themselves dictated the form of each line and cadence: syllabic stresses and speech patterns were not to be twisted into mere tunefulness at the expense of sense. With the approach of the Second World War, Finzi's uncompromising music was a perfect match for the words of F. L. Lucas's prophetic 'June on Castle Hill', and even more powerful was his setting of Thomas Hardy's 'Channel Firing'.

Hardy appealed greatly to Finzi. He published three sets of songs for voice and piano taken from Hardy's poems – *A Young Man's Exhortation, Earth and Air and Rain,* and *Before and After Summer* – and after his death other single items were brought together. Gloucestershire had prompted *A Severn Rhapsody,* but he was to withdraw this for revision. His interest was drawn elsewhere: the somewhat complacent prettiness of Painswick had less to offer him than the sterner territories of Hardy's own countryside and Hardy's pessimistic temperament.

4
Wessex and the South Country

And they felt old muscles travel
Over their tense contours,
And with long skill unravel
Cunningest scores.
Thomas Hardy
(from 'A Phantasy in a
Museum of Musical Instruments')

In 1913, Edward Elgar and Thomas Hardy were brought together by a mutual friend with a view to their collaborating on an opera. Both were willing, and among favoured subjects were Hardy's novels *The Trumpet Major* and *The Return of the Native*, and his epic poem *The Dynasts*. Nothing came of the plan, but those three themes and many other related scenes have attracted and continue to attract other composers. Hardy's world, sombre as it may have been, is still pulsating with life.

On 1st April 1981, Alun Hoddinott's opera *The Trumpet Major* had its première, and in the issue of *The Sunday Times* which reported this there was also a review of George Nicholson's recent setting of a Hardy poem, *The Convergence of the Twain*. Gustav Holst's favourite among his own works was the tone poem *Egdon Heath*, and although nobody has yet tackled a full-scale setting of *The Dynasts*, Thomas Dunhill at least made a fine male chorus out of the 'Song of the King's Men'.

Baron Frédéric d'Erlanger, a banker and largely self-taught composer who insisted on retaining his French title after becoming a naturalized Englishman, wrote an opera, *Tess*, on the story of *Tess of the d'Urbervilles*, but it seems unlikely that this will ever be revived at Covent Garden or anywhere else. Innumerable settings of individual poems, however, continue to be performed. When he was a student under Stanford at the RCM, Arthur Bliss presented his tutor with a setting of *The Dark-eyed Gentleman*, whose arch reminiscence of a man who had tied up a lady's garter and given her an illegitimate son was not at all to the professor's taste: he angrily ordered Bliss to take this unpleasant poem away from his desk. Rutland Boughton based his opera *The Queen of Cornwall* on Hardy's play, and Henry Balfour Gardiner took his frequently played *Shepherd Fennel's Dance* from a character in one of the *Wessex Tales*.

Balfour Gardiner, for a while music master at Winchester College, was a composer of great taste and sensitivity, but not one whose works are likely to achieve immortality. His own modest awareness of the greater genius of some of his friends and contemporaries remains one of the most attractive things about him. He sponsored series of concerts of modern British music and paid for the production of several works by Bax, Holst and Percy Grainger: Grainger spoke of his 'endless life-saving generosity to fellow composers'. On his extensive estates near Ashmore in Dorset, Gardiner planted woods and coppices named after his friends – for instance, the Gustav Plantation. And it was he who organized the first performance of *The Planets* at the Queen's Hall in London for the composer's friends and others who could be hastily encouraged to attend, before Holst left for service abroad in the First World War.

Gustav Holst, like Elgar, met Hardy personally, but with more fruitful results. Although by 1920 the author was frail and had only a couple of years to live, he was delighted to accompany Holst over Winfrith Heath and share the mysteries and secret music of what in his novels had become 'Egdon Heath'. Holst felt himself at once in tune with the haggard, brooding expanse of land, and promised himself that in a few years he would produce a work of some kind to reflect the elements which Hardy had captured in the opening pages of *The Return of the Native*:

> Intensity was more usually reached by way of the solemn than by way of the brilliant, and such a sort of intensity was often arrived at during winter darkness, tempests, and mists. Then Egdon was aroused to reciprocity; for the storm was its lover, and the wind its friend. Then it became the home of strange phantoms; and it was found to be the hitherto unrecognized original of those wild regions of obscurity which are vaguely felt to be compassing us about in midnight dreams of flight and disaster, and are never thought of after the dream till revived by scenes like this.

Holst found himself indeed encompassed about by the subject, which drove other projects out of his mind and refused to be postponed. By the end of July 1927 he had done a considerable amount of work on it and was ready to re-visit the scene itself. He spent a long weekend tramping from Bristol to Dorchester, where Hardy gave him lunch and showed him around other places featured in the sequence of novels on which the old county name of Wessex had been bestowed.

Both agreed that winter was the best time of year to get the fullest value from the heath, when it was agitated by the 'worn whisper' of dried grasses and flowers. After opening his piece on muted double basses to establish the brooding, 'swarthy monotony', as Hardy wrote in a line quoted by Holst at the head of the score, the composer soon caught this interminable fretting of the wind in several rustling string passages. The sub-title reads 'Homage to Thomas Hardy', but sadly the novelist did not live to hear *Egdon Heath*: the first performance did not come until February 1928, a few weeks too late.

More recently, Richard Rodney Bennett provided atmospheric music for the film version of *Far From the Madding Crowd*. His score interweaves human characters with themes depicting landscape, weather, and the changing seasons. No sympathizer with the folk song conservationist school, Bennett used the outlines of original folk tunes to suit his own purposes whilst never over-decorating them. Most of the melodies come, appropriately enough, from western England; but Vaughan Williams's old Essex favourite, 'Bushes and Briars', crops up at one stage.

Another grim place which appealed to Thomas Hardy was the great hill fort of Maiden Castle, south of Dorchester. With four rings of massive ramparts stepped up along the contours of the hill, this ancient religious and defensive site covers more than a hundred acres, and the perimeter of its inner camp is about a mile and a half round. Stone Age and Iron Age occupants and visiting worshippers fought against successive invasions of different Celtic tribes, until in the end the fortress fell to the Romans. Sir Mortimer Wheeler's skilful sectionalized excavations in 1934 revealed the different layers of different cultures, the vast stores of stones brought from Chesil Beach as sling-shot, and the ashes and broken bodies of the final massacre.

Many years before Sir Mortimer disinterred all its secrets, Hardy had written of the mighty earthwork under the Celtic name of Mai-Dun. It was under this title that John Ireland completed a symphonic rhapsody in 1921, leavening the clash of military conflict and recurrent brass calls to battle with reflective interludes. As we noted earlier, Ireland shared Housman's ironic pessimism about the world, and he found another kindred spirit in the fatalistic Hardy, believing not in a loving Christian deity but in a 'President of the Immortals' who treated mankind as an offhanded, rather pathetic joke.

Grim echoes of a prehistoric past always argued in Ireland's mind with wistful intimations of lost beauty. *Mai-Dun* is filled with brutality and terror; but at other times he would try to conjure up a vision of simpler, happier ghosts. The Channel Islands and Sussex were to offer him the most direct inspiration.

Born at Bowden in Cheshire in 1879, John Ireland was the youngest of five children. Bullied by the older ones and so unhappy at boarding school that he ran back home, only to be locked up and maltreated by his sisters, he found his only real escape in music. Just after his fourteenth birthday he was accepted by the RCM as a piano student and later as an organ student, and before the age of sixteen became the youngest FRCO in history.

Soon after he arrived in London his parents died, leaving him enough money to provide a small income, strictly meted out by two guardians, which had to be supplemented by accompanying singers at smoking concerts, or Charles Coborn of 'Two Lovely Black Eyes' fame at the Holborn Restaurant, and by playing the organ. In 1896 he was appointed assistant organist to Holy Trinity, Sloane Street, then organist at St Jude's and at St Luke's, Chelsea, where he remained until 1926. His home for many years was in Gunter Grove, Chelsea, but although church duties and, after 1923, his duties as Professor of Composition at the RCM, kept him mainly in London, he travelled whenever he could get away to prehistoric sites which awoke strange resonances in him.

In 1906 he had made the acquaintance of the mystical, magical tales of the Welsh novelist Arthur Machen, and was soon to become his devoted friend and admirer. They shared a sort of pagan belief in 'racial memory', and Ireland strove to find an expressive musical counterpart to Machen's prose, in which 'lay hidden the secret of the sensuous art of literature ... the secret of suggestion, the art of causing delicious sensation by the use of words'. Machen's secrets and sensations were those of an occult world, sometimes entrancing and sometimes ominous; of something not yet dead in ancient tombs and standing stones, of ancient religions and timeless hills of dreams. It was a world which John Ireland was to visit regularly.

While staying in Jersey in 1913 he began work on *The Forgotten Rite*, a tone poem largely inspired by the neolithic dolmens of the Channel Islands such as La Hougue Bie which lie almost exactly halfway between Stonehenge in Wiltshire and Carnac in Brittany. The music begins with a rumble of distant thunder – or is it some supernatural stirring of a creature waking from centuries of neglect, turning over, and drowsing again? Spacious chords suggest a sinister organ chorale; then there is a hint of the sea, a suggestively pagan horn soliloquy, and a sudden romantic outburst, conjuring up a turbulent ancient rite and then letting the echoes die away into limbo once more. It is not so much programme music as atavistic music, luring us into remembering our own dreams and at the same time submerging us in the slow swell of shared racial memory.

Around the same time, and in the same vein, Ireland wrote a set of piano pieces, including *The Island Spell*. His friend and biographer John Longmire tells of an odd hitch in completing this work. The original idea came to Ireland while he was swimming, and when he got back to his holiday flat he sketched it out but could not reach a satisfactory resolution of the final section. Back home in Chelsea he made several attempts, but it was not until he returned to Jersey and bathed at the same hour of the day from the same beach that the closing bars came unbidden but quite clear into his mind.

It is difficult to believe without reservation in Ireland's claim, made late in life, that 'At the time many of my works were published, publishers liked titles – they didn't care how they were invented, so long as there were titles', and that this was his only reason for calling them what he did rather than simply classifying them as Intermezzi, Nocturnes, Ballades and so on. 'Music means only itself,' he insisted. But whatever his disclaimers, the pictorial element remains unmistakably there: a synthesis of the real and the imaginary into his own fantastic landscape, so beautifully accomplished that it has led to his being aptly described as 'an epic miniaturist'.

Alan Bush, a composition pupil of Ireland who often heard the composer playing his own work, declares that Ireland's melodic style is purely English, but that his harmonic vocabulary, though essentially English, is often enriched from German chromaticism of the late nineteenth century and sometimes from more recent French impressionists.

John Ireland returned to the Channel Islands shortly before the outbreak of the Second World War. He settled with John Longmire on Guernsey in a house called

Fort Saumarez, near the Martello tower of L'Erée, and was shaping up ideas for a piano suite called *Sarnia* when war came. Sarnia was the Latin name for the island, and the three movements of the suite depict various moods of nature on Guernsey whilst, typically, capturing the mystical undertones of the region. The first invokes Le Catorioc, a place on which stands a large dolmen rumoured to have been the centre of witches' sabbaths and earlier dark rites. Appended to it is a quotation from an old text, used also in one of Machen's novels:

> All day long, heavy silence broods, and a certain hidden terror lurks there. But at nightfall gleams the light of fires . . . the shrilling of flutes and the clash of cymbals re-echo . . .

The second movement, *In a May Morning*, carries a quotation from Victor Hugo, who lived on the island between 1855 and 1870 after being banished from France by Louis Napoleon and then from Jersey because of his political activities. Ireland himself once begged an admirer to play this piece 'as though you were imagining something so lovely you could hardly bear it'. Alan Bush has spoken of John Ireland's inheritance, via his professor at the RCM, of the classical European style in direct descent from Clara Schumann; and to me there are indefinable resemblances in mood and texture between *In a May Morning* and the *Spring Song* of Schumann's Opus 68; but this may be only a personal reaction. The third section, a swirling *Song of the Spring Tides*, quotes Swinburne.

Work on the suite was interrupted by the threat of German invasion and had to be completed in England after Ireland had fled on one of the last boats to leave Guernsey. He returned in 1947 for a visit, hoping to settle permanently, but because of tax problems and a general disillusionment with the post-war scene this never came about. Instead, he turned his attention to another of his favourite regions. In 1949 he took a flat in a farmhouse near Ashington in Sussex, and ultimately bought a converted windmill nearby, Rock Mill, which was to be his home for the rest of his days.

Sussex had already stimulated him many times to composition. In 1921 a piano piece, *Amberley Wild Brooks*, portrayed the convolutions of those meandering little waterways which in winter can flood the levels about Amberley village but at other times of year charm with their ripples and glinting lights. Ireland's writing suggests in the right hand the sparkle and eddy of these ripples against their banks, while arpeggios in the left hand roll like a wider, more purposeful current.

In the autumn of 1922 there are reflections of those rippling figures in *Equinox*, another piano piece. This time the flurries are those of a slowly gathering gale which the composer experienced while walking on the Downs. Not for the first time we sense some invisible force deeper than everyday natural phenomena: a deep tumult rising from the bass to toss clouds and wind currents about in growing fury.

On Monkton Down in the west of Sussex is a group of six large bell barrows known as the Devil's Jumps, one of them the highest barrow in the county. These inspired the slow movement of the Sonata for Cello and Piano in 1924. Starting

Amberley Wild Brooks, Sussex.

Within the ancient hill-fort and beech trees of Chanctonbury Ring,
on whose slopes John Ireland encountered dancing children from another era.

with a gentle piano soliloquy, this sombre yet somehow life-enhancing movement dreams between the vehemence of the first movement and the aggressive outbursts of the last. At the time of composing, Ireland was reading William Blake's *Heaven and Hell*, whose contrasts between delight and despair appealed to much in his own temperament and find a parallel in much of his music of this period. For myself, whenever I am in that region I find that the sonata comes into my head not near Monkton Down but in the secretive, haunted Kingley Vale, with its shadowy yew forest and the barrows of the Devil's Humps.

It is highly appropriate that the *Legend* for piano and orchestra of 1933 should be dedicated to Arthur Machen. During one of his long creative spells at Ashington, Ireland had gone walking on Harrow Hill, just the sort of place to appeal to him with the shafts and dumps of its neolithic flint mines, the outline of a small fort probably dating from the early Iron Age, and remains of a small church. This church once sheltered a leper colony, and meditations upon the path known as Lepers' Way inspired the first and last sections of the *Legend*. The central section has a more remarkable origin, however. Walking up a different slope towards his favourite sight of all, Chanctonbury Ring, Ireland had a sudden vision of a group of dancing children. Their old-fashioned dress was not of this age; and he realized that their nimble footsteps made no sound whatsoever. Yet he claimed afterwards that he had actually talked to them before, as suddenly as they had appeared, they vanished. One of Arthur Machen's stories is built around just such an occurrence. Between the two friends, which was the fiction and which the truth that kindled the fiction?

In 1939, before leaving for what he misguidedly hoped would be the peace of Guernsey, Ireland started his moving *Concertino Pastorale* for strings while staying further along the south coast at Deal. Already saddened by the relentless approach of war, and foreseeing the death of the rural peace he most cherished, he put his heart into the work. The lilting first movement is interrupted by melancholy little asides, which presage the threnody of the second movement, a lament for all that was most beautiful and tranquil in life. In this movement are many of those aspiring phrases so characteristic of Ireland – a rising, yearning line which fatalistically falls a sad third, fourth, fifth or even a whole octave just when it seems most confident of reaching its zenith. The final driving toccata is almost spiteful and dismissive, as if the composer were brutally scorning his own nostalgia.

While staying in Sussex after the war, Ireland frequently met his friend Sir Arnold Bax, since 1941 Master of the King's Musick, at The White Horse in Storrington, and, since Bax had no car, drove him about the region, trying to convey his own affection for it to the Celtic-obsessed Bax.

In 1953 he left London for good to settle into Rock Mill, with an uninterrupted view of Chanctonbury Ring and a great sweep of the Downs. Only a few yards along a narrow lane escaping from the pounding traffic of the A24 into Worthing, the mill today is surrounded by machinery and the yawning chasms of the Windmill Sandpit, perched on its wooded knoll like some medieval keep providing a last refuge on the motte of its devastated castle.

Rock Mill, John Ireland's last home in Sussex.

When John Ireland's sight began to deteriorate, he grew unwilling to travel far or communicate with anyone other than his closest friends; though on his eighty-second birthday he was persuaded to attend a concert in his honour in London – his last public appearance. He died in 1962 and was buried at his own wish in the churchyard of the little village of Shipley. On a plaque set in a sarsen stone, threatened with engulfment by the thick hedge behind it, is the epitaph: 'One of God's noblest works lies here.' Whether Ireland himself, with his mistrust of the conduct of the President of the Immortals, would altogether have approved of such wording, we do not know. But we do know he wanted to be buried within sight of Chanctonbury Ring, and so he is – or, rather, he is so during the winter. In summer the trees between are so richly decked with leaves that one has to walk to the farther side of the churchyard to see the Ring. But there it is, watching over one of its great lovers.

Shipley also has its mill, for long the home of Hilaire Belloc. One of Belloc's poems about the region, 'Ha'naker Mill' – Halnaker being still there, nicely restored, not far outside Chichester – was set to music by Peter Warlock and by Ivor Gurney.

Hubert Parry, born in Bournemouth in February 1848, shared his time when not teaching at the RCM, of which he became director in 1894, between the family estate at Highnam in Gloucestershire and a house he had bought at Rustington in Sussex. Highnam Court, two miles west of Gloucester off the A40, had originally belonged to the abbey of Gloucester, but after Henry VIII had granted it to one of his supporters it was handed down through various marriages and inheritors until it was bought in 1837 by Thomas Gambier-Parry, Hubert's father. Hubert inherited in 1896, by which time he had come to know everyone on the estate. His bailiff later reminisced about Parry's habit of taking out his tuning fork whenever he heard a cuckoo and making a note of the pitch and interval. One year when he was too busy to get to Highnam at the right time of year he asked the bailiff's wife to listen on his behalf, pick out the notes on the piano, and keep a record of the dates. On another occasion Parry requested one of his oldest employees to sing a traditional country tune so that he could take it down, but the old man was stricken so dumb when his master was looking at him that the only way to get him to sing was to take him into a pitch-dark shed, after which Parry dashed away and scribbled the notes down on paper as quickly as possible before he could forget them.

In 1898 Hubert Parry, perhaps best remembered now for his ode *Blest Pair of Sirens*, and by young piano duettists for his settings of *Popular Tunes of the British Isles*, was knighted; and in the same year his daughter married Arthur Ponsonby, in the Diplomatic Service at Copenhagen. When the Ponsonbys returned to England it was to settle in the family house of Shulbrede Priory in Sussex, in wooded country between Linchmere and Fernhurst. Parry loved to visit them here, and wrote a piano suite of *Shulbrede Tunes*, with glimpses here and there of neatly turned quotations from nursery rhymes.

During the last weeks of his life he was staying at Rustington, resting after strenuous war work and repeated attacks of severe lumbago. In spite of the pain

Shulbrede Priory, home of the Ponsonby family, for whom Sir Hubert Parry
wrote his *Shulbrede Tunes*.

Pen Pits below Arthur Bliss's home.

he enjoyed taking long cycle rides through the Sussex countryside, and indulged in a particularly extended one on 6th September 1918. When he got back a protruberance developed in his groin, his strength ebbed swiftly away, and on 7th October he died from blood poisoning, thought to be the result of a rupture caused during that last cycle ride. He had never feared death itself but, according to Herbert Howells, was concerned about what would befall the Highnam estate after he was gone: might not his successors cut down some of his favourite, irreplaceable trees?

Sir Hubert Parry was buried in St Paul's, and there is also a memorial tablet in Gloucester Cathedral with an epitaph written by Robert Bridges, who had been with Parry at Eton and for some of whose poems Parry had supplied his most personally committed music – *Invocation to Music* and *Song of Darkness and Light* among them. It was Bridges who had first suggested that his friend should write 'suitable, simple music' to Blake's 'Jerusalem'; then, when nothing came of it, thought George Butterworth might undertake the task. Butterworth did not live to do so, and it was not until the spring of 1918 that *Jerusalem* made its mark at an Albert Hall concert in celebration of the success of the campaign for women's suffrage, of which Parry had long been an ardent supporter.

Another keen cyclist and country wanderer, Edward Elgar, also knew the remote ways of Sussex. In 1917 his wife found a thatched cottage, Brinkwells, near Fittleworth. It was small and lonely and notably lacking in any amenities, but Elgar was delighted with the view over the river Arun to the Downs, and the seclusion of the woods through which he could walk uninterrupted. He spent more time chopping wood for the fire and learning to make hoops for barrels than he did working in his garden studio; but it was here that he managed happily to complete his Cello Concerto. After his wife's death and before his daughter's marriage he spent a whole summer at Brinkwells, though without composing a single bar. The cottage is still there and still sounding with music: at the time of writing, its occupant is the composer Robert Walker, one of the artistic directors of the Petworth Festival.

Sir Arthur Bliss, who became Master of the Queen's Music in 1953 after the death of Bax, has a worthy memorial in Sussex.

Son of an American father, and himself destined to marry an American girl, Bliss was born in 1891 in a house beside Barnes Common which was bombed in the Second World War. His own first recorded memory is of earlier devastation – watching gorse bushes ablaze from his bedroom window. After a spell in America and his marriage there, he brought his wife to London, but in 1933 found a country home for themselves and their two daughters at Pen Pits near Stourhead in Somerset, with a view of Salisbury Plain. The pits referred to are craters up to thirty feet in diameter, which may have been relics of prehistoric flint mines; and there are local legends of the site having been used as a camp during a battle against the Danes in AD 879, from which derives Alfred's Tower, erected in 1772 by the Hoare family of Stourhead. Bliss was evidently not impelled by these surroundings to compose any stirring epic or song cycle, but worked happily at Pen Pits – on compositions including his film score for H. G. Wells's *Shape of*

St Paul's church, Elsted, dating from the time of Edward the Confessor and
known to the madrigalist Thomas Weelkes, whose father was rector
there for many years.

Things to Come – until after the Second World War, when he had to return
permanently to London.

During the war he had begun work in the Department of Overseas Music of the
BBC, and became Director of Music between 1942 and 1944. Within a short time
of taking up this task he had also taken the measure of BBC music policy well
enough to prepare a document on future options which included some
remarkably accurate predictions, not least his declaration that the ideal method
of broadcasting would be to have three separate channels from which 'all citizens
worth fighting for' would have two contrasting programmes to provide
sustenance at any minute of the day, while for 'the Calibans' there would be 'a
"dirt track", a continual stream of noise and nonsense put on by untouchables
with the use of records'. How prophetic!

In 1962, in acknowledgment of his successful ballet *Checkmate* and his own
devotion to the game of chess, Bliss was invited to make the opening move in the
annual Hastings and St Leonards Chess Congress.

The following year he was visiting Sussex again, this time to bestow his name
on an even worthier cause. The Samaritan Housing Association, which aimed to

provide homes for old people where they could keep in close touch with their families, planned a group of such houses at Lindfield which would be named after living musicians. The chairman asked Sir Arthur to lay the foundation stone of the first, Arthur Bliss House, with two similar residences, Yehudi Menuhin House and Malcolm Sargent House, to follow.

His last major work, *Shield of Faith*, for soprano, baritone, choir and organ, was written in 1975 for the quincentenary of St George's Chapel, Windsor.

Going back in history but not too far in space, we come to the village of Elsted between Midhurst and Petersfield. Other places such as Ripon, and the counties of Cheshire and Hampshire, claim without much evidence to have been the birthplace of the most daring and original of English madrigal composers; but the likeliest story is that Thomas Weelkes was born in Elsted rectory in October 1576, his father then being rector there and remaining so until his death in 1597.

Early in the young Thomas's musical career he seems to have been attached to the household of the 'Right Worshipful George Phillpot Esquire', to whom his first volume of madrigals was dedicated in the year of his father's death. The family seat of the Phillpots was at Thruxton near Andover, but George Phillpot is known to have lived at Compton Place near Twyford church, another of John Weelkes's incumbencies in the Winchester diocese.

By the end of 1598 Thomas was appointed organist at Winchester College, and a few years later went to Chichester Cathedral as organist, *informator choristarum*, and Sherborne Clerk, this third being a lay singer's post with a stipend of some consequence.

His first volume of twenty-four madrigals for different consorts of voices had shown a much more adventurous style than any of his predecessors. Rich in harmonic and contrapuntal experiment, they must have startled contemporaries with such devices as discordant clashes between simultaneous major and minor thirds. A second volume of *Balletts and Madrigals* followed, and then a third set including the dramatic *Thule, the period of cosmography*, a sort of awestruck guide to Iceland and other spectacular regions and sights of which sixteenth-century travellers had brought back news to their countrymen. There are volcanoes like Etna, and Hekla with its 'sulphureous fire'; a colourful musical canvas of another volcano in Tierra del Fuego; oceans alive with flying fishes. One cannot but be struck by the incongruity of this provincial musician in cloistered surroundings letting fly with such fantasies of far-off lands, and in such exploratively chromatic language.

Weelkes was soon so highly esteemed by fellow madrigalists that in 1601 he was invited by Thomas Morley to contribute to *The Triumphs of Oriana*, an anthology issued in honour of the ageing Queen Elizabeth. In February, at All Saints' church, Chichester, he married the daughter of a prosperous local merchant, and, with his reputation as a composer and his tripartite income from the cathedral, seemed all set for a comfortable career. Unfortunately, however, he seems to have taken to the bottle. Apparently he was not alone in this – official reports after formal visitations to the cathedral lay considerable stress on the inefficiency, drunkenness and persistent absenteeism of numbers of the staff. In fact, the situation became so blatant that in 1610 a decree was issued enjoining church officials 'not to frequent tippling houses'.

In a drunken state, the reasons for which we cannot profitably seek at this remove, Weelkes became involved in a lawsuit with his own wife and mother-in-law, was taken to task by his Bishop for drunkenness and negligence, and early in 1617 was dismissed from his cathedral posts on the grounds that 'he hath been and is noted for a common drunkard and a notorious swearer and blasphemer'. His replacement could not have been too satisfactory, for Weelkes soon reappeared at the organ; but he still indulged in his old habits and, according to William Lawes in 1619:

> divers times and very often comes so disguised either from the tavern
> or alehouse into the choir as is much to be lamented, for in these
> humours he will both curse and swear most dreadfully, and so
> profane the service of God (and especially on the Sabbath days) as is
> most fearful to hear, and to the great amazement of the people
> present.

His wife died in September 1622, and Weelkes survived her only a year, dying during a visit to London while staying with a friend whose surname, Drinkwater, ought to have had more influence on him. He was buried in St Bride's, Fleet Street, close to the Bride Lane tavern in which the first meetings of the London Madrigal Society were to be held just over a century later. In the north aisle of Chichester Cathedral he is included, despite his transgressions while serving there, among a series of stained glass portraits of eminent divines and other people associated with the building's history.

Sussex has sheltered more visitors and settlers than indigenous musicians. A composer who spent most of his creative years here came originally from Dresden in Staffordshire, now part of Stoke-on-Trent. Havergal Brian, born 1876, studied music somewhat spasmodically at Birmingham but was largely self-taught, and as prickly and wayward as many such composers are. In 1919 he took a tiny flat in St Anne's Crescent, Lewes, attracted to the place by a vision he had had years before. In a dream he had seen a towered and turreted city which, for some reason, he associated with the name of Nuremberg. When walking on the Downs, he set eyes for the first time on Lewes, and found that it corresponded in nearly every detail to his dream city.

From this sprang a symphony on which Brian was to work intensively after he and his wife and family, in financial straits which he was too proud to admit openly, had moved into a council house at Moulsecoomb, on the outskirts of Brighton. He had already shown his affection for the county in the Sussex pastoral scenes of his *Third English Suite*, and in April 1921 his first symphony had been performed on the West Pier. In a programme note for a recent Brighton Festival, Gavin Henderson records that the flamboyant Lyell-Taylor, before conducting this work, told the audience that as they could not expect to understand a new work so far above their heads at first hearing he proposed to repeat it at every concert that week and twice on Saturday. But this work is not now listed as Havergal Brian's First: that numbering is reserved for his huge *Gothic Symphony*, the largest piece of its kind in history, calling for an orchestra of 200, four brass bands, and 500 singers plus four soloists and an organ. It owed its inception to the Lewes experience and Brian's love of wind and weather on the Downs – though in fits of irritation he was known to declare 'the South is too slow and too sleepy'.

The *Gothic* built up between 1919 and 1927, most of it being written in 1922, but it was not performed until 1961, and then mainly thanks to the efforts of the conductor Bryan Fairfax and the composer Robert Simpson. Such neglect might depress Havergal Brian, but it did not stop him composing. By 1968 he had reached Symphony 32, which was performed in London in 1971. He had by this time been living for almost five years at Atlantic Court in Shoreham, still working but growing increasingly deaf and unsteady on his feet. On 13th November 1972 he left his flat to post a letter, for once forgetting to take his walking stick. On his return he missed his usual entrance and fell down an unexpected step. Bruised and dizzy, he was taken to hospital: pneumonia set in, and fifteen days after his fall he was dead. On the day of his cremation his children got a shock: they learned for the first time that Havergal Brian had been married before, in his early years in the Potteries, and that there had been five children by the first marriage.

Generations of a less complicated musical family have lived for over 200 years in and around Saltdean, Ovingdean, Woodingdean and Rottingdean. So many of them are buried in one part of Rottingdean churchyard that it became known locally as 'Coppers' Corner'. The Coppers had always been singers, long before there was any conscious 'folk movement', and many of their tunes and verses, passed on orally as a family tradition, were in due course written down by Jim Copper, who died in 1854. These books remain in the possession of Bob Copper, who has himself written a number of books about their background, including the award-winning *A Song for Every Season*.

The songs deal with every aspect of village and Downland life, and occasionally with the fishermen of the Channel coast. There are songs of courtship and a few historical memories, but mainly the tale is of the farming routine – the life of the shepherd, sheep-shearing, ploughing, threshing, and the gaiety of seasonal celebrations. Everything is dramatic, direct, and sharply observed: who could ever forget the picture of the birds singing on a spray in 'By the Green Grove'? The Coppers have played an influential part in the folk song revival of our own time.

Other voices sing other parts in a cleft of the Downs east of Lewes. In a Sussex history of 1835 the house of Glynde Bourne is described as 'a neat but unpretending edifice, once a favourite abode of the Muses'. About a century later it was again to be favoured by the Muses. In 1931 John Christie, owner of the estate, married the soprano Audrey Mildmay and was seized by the idea of building a small opera house in which they could mount productions of works best suited to her voice. Christie himself was in favour of a Wagner festival, but his wife preferred Mozart, and in the end it was Mozart who became the presiding genius, though other composers were to be added as the years went on.

Glyndebourne, with a glimpse of the opera house roof beyond the main house.

At the end of 1933 Christie visited Copenhagen to see if he could arouse the interest of the conductor Fritz Busch. The first actual performance that winter was, however, given under Boyd Neel. The theatre was almost finished and preliminary acoustic tests were being made when Christie suddenly suggested that a proper performance should be put on for the benefit of an audience of friends. There were in fact two sessions in one day: the Intimate Opera Company and the Boyd Neel Orchestra presented a programme of two one-act operas, *La Serva Padrone* and *Bastien und Bastienne*, and a dramatized version of Bach's *Coffee Cantata*.

Some newspapers grumbled about the engagement of foreign musicians such as Fritz Busch and Carl Ebert for the eventual running of the opera, and the music critic of the *Morning Post*, learning that Mr Christie was pricing his seats at £2 each, commented: 'Unless his performances are of the first order this would seem to be a lot of money and, in any event, a sum which comparatively few would or could pay.'

The completed theatre opened on 28th May 1934 with Audrey Mildmay as Susanna in what Rossini called 'the finest possible masterpiece of musical comedy' – *Le Nozze di Figaro*. On the second evening only seven people showed up. By the fourth night every seat was sold out, and the scene has rarely been otherwise since. During the Second World War the opera house became a children's home, but reopened in 1946 with Benjamin Britten's *The Rape of Lucretia*.

Although one has to leave London by train or car in the early afternoon, the convention of the occasion has always demanded evening dress, making an odd sight on station platforms but a pretty sight along the walks and by the luxuriant flowerbeds of Glyndebourne. Perhaps the performances are in danger of becoming social occasions rather than musical events. I have a fond memory of an office girl in a London firm I once worked for who, baffled that I should have gone to listen to 'a lot of lah-lah-lah in Eyetalian' at Glyndebourne, insisted that 'people only go there to be seen'. After I had tried to defend the musical rather than snobbish aspects of the place, she summed up with what I still regard as the most succinct appraisal of opera I have ever heard: 'Well, I s'pose it's like beer – tastes horrible the first time you try it, but if you have enough you get used to it.'

Moving eastwards from the Sussex Downs, I once caught a glimpse of a name and titles which might or might not be interesting. It is hard to guess, since there was no accompanying sound. In 1926 an overture called *The Kentish Downs* by Susan Spain-Dunk was performed at a Promenade Concert. The lady reappeared the following year, in the first Prom season under the aegis of the BBC, with an orchestral poem *Elaine*. But when did any of us last hear anything of her?

The brick keep of Tattershall Castle, Lincolnshire, all that remains of the
fortified moated house built by Ralph Cromwell, Lord Treasurer, in 1433.
John Taverner held a benefice in the collegiate church and wrote masses,
motets and songs before becoming an agent of Thomas Cromwell and
forsaking music.

5
East Anglia

Here joyless roam a wild amphibious race,
With sullen wo displayed in every face;
Who far from civil arts and social fly,
And scowl at strangers with suspicious eye.
George Crabbe

The Fenlands and the old counties and borderlands of the Angles have bred a tough strain of dissenters throughout many reigns, even before the time when Oliver Cromwell rallied the forces of the Eastern Association against Charles I. Some of the Puritan Pilgrim Fathers were imprisoned in Boston. Robert Kett from Wymondham led a rebellion against land enclosures and at one stage seized the city of Norwich. The 'Fenland Tigers' fought every attempt to drain the meres on the grounds that this would deprive them of their living from fishing and wildfowling. Musicians shared many of these stubborn refusals to conform, either as puritans or recusants; though some, putting their craft above their conscience, found ways of talking themselves into compliance.

John Taverner, thought to have been born in 1495 at Tattershall in southern Lincolnshire (and not to be confused with the composer of similar name born in London in 1944) held for some years a benefice in the collegiate church there. He left in 1526 for an appointment by Cardinal Wolsey as *informator choristarum* at what was then Cardinal College, now Christ Church, Oxford. Two years later he became involved in a group of Lutheran heretics and was imprisoned until in 1530 Wolsey, needing his services, arranged for a pardon. He returned to Lincolnshire, this time settling in Boston and duly adjusting his religious persuasions to suit Thomas Cromwell, whose agent he became in suppression of four friaries and the fanatical persecution of 'idolaters'. He died in 1545, having abandoned music: but is remembered less for his later tyrannies than for the beauty of his eight masses, especially *The Western Wynde*, in which a shred of folk song is built up by free variations into a grand design speaking eloquently of the English countryside.

Another Lincolnshire man, William Byrd, studied under Thomas Tallis and at twenty years of age became organist at Lincoln Cathedral. Their eventual joint control of music printing under Elizabeth I was somewhat surprising in that Byrd continued to be a 'Popish recusant' – though not too wholeheartedly, since he shared organ duties during Chapel Royal services with Tallis. He composed

83

sacred and secular music, masses and madrigals, as cheerfully for the Anglican church as for the Roman; and died in his eightieth year on his country estate at Stondon Massey in Essex, where a memorial stone is set in the church wall.

Epworth rectory, once in Lincolnshire but now designated as Humberside, was the birthplace of John Wesley, founder of Methodism, and his younger brother Charles, who was to write not just hundreds but thousands of hymns in the Methodist cause, including *Jesu, lover of my Soul*. His son Charles was also a considerable performer and composer.

Percy Grainger was at work long before anyone thought of redefining and misnaming the counties of England. One doubts if he would have fancied bunching a Humberside posy. As it is, *A Lincolnshire Posy* preserves a number of traditional old tunes, including the tale of the 'brisk young sailor', arranged for piano duet and also in a splendid version for brass. In 1905 at Redbourne, also now in Humberside, he recorded 'I'm Seventeen come Sunday', one of those 'fal-diddle-ay-do' ditties which can go so wrong and lend themselves so easily to parody. In 1908 Joseph Taylor of Brigg sang for him the unforgettable 'Brigg Fair', and after producing a setting of his own, Grainger passed it on with characteristic generosity to Delius, who was to put it to quite a different use.

An earlier collector of rural airs, perhaps the first truly influential one, was John Playford, born in Norfolk in 1623. He went to London in his mid-twenties to establish himself as a bookseller and music publisher, and two years later published *The English Dancing Master*, a comprehensive collection of country dance tunes for the violin. Some of his pieces have been rearranged by Herbert Howells.

We have seen how Vaughan Williams began his collection of folk songs in Essex. He soon moved deeper into the eastern counties, finding songs in and around King's Lynn, many of them old fishermen's ditties, and blending them into three *Norfolk Rhapsodies*. At about the same time he was working on another orchestral piece called *In the Fen Country*, which he revised a couple of times before publishing in 1907: this time he did not use actual folk tunes but created his own themes in the same mood. Just before leaving for Paris to study with Ravel he made another trip to Norfolk, this time to collect tunes from the Broads.

There may have seemed to be little incentive for developing a musical culture in the waterlogged, inhospitable Fens, but some of the monks and hermits on their damp island refuges are reputed to have made a gladsome sound. An old ballad telling of King Canute's survey of the brackish region by barge reports:

> Merrily sang they, the monks at Ely,
> When Canut the King he rowed thereby;
> Row to the shore, men, said the King,
> And let us hear these monks to sing.

Around 1500, Christopher Tye was born on that same island. First a choirboy at King's College Chapel in Cambridge, he then became a lay clerk there. In 1541 he was appointed choirmaster at Ely Cathedral, and is thought to have been music

Vaughan Williams's *In the Fen Country* conjures up the reedy lodes and
droves of peatland such as Wicken Sedge Fen, preserved in its natural
state by the National Trust.

This house was once the Windmill Inn at Stalham in Norfolk, frequented by
Peter Warlock and E. J. Moeran during their quests for local folk songs, and
close to the *Stalham River* of Moeran's tone poem.

master to Edward VI between 1544 and 1550, becoming also a Gentleman of the Chapel Royal. In 1561 he resigned from the cathedral, was ordained, and in due course held three livings in the Isle of Ely, his main base being at Doddington, near March. He left both verse and music, including masses, motets and anthems, and metrical settings of the Acts of the Apostles.

Norfolk meant a great deal to E. J. Moeran, who was born at Heston in Middlesex on the last day of 1894 but whose father came from Norfolk and during Ernest's childhood held a living there. Moeran felt some ancestral tug towards the county and, although in the end he settled in Herefordshire, a great deal of his music is coloured by his repeated visits collecting Norfolk and Suffolk folk songs. One day in 1921 he jotted down words and melody sung in a pub at Cley-next-the-Sea by a John Drinkwater – not the poet of that name – and drew them to the attention of his friend Peter Warlock. This became the song we now know as *Yarmouth Fair*, though hardly in its original form. The words they first heard proved to be those of a published piece called *The Magpie said 'Come In'*, and permission to use this copyright material with Drinkwater's tune was refused. Warlock and Moeran turned to a mutual friend, Hal Collins, to provide the lyrics we now know.

Moeran himself composed *Stalham River* and *Windmills*, reflecting features of the Norfolk landscape. In 1935 he used a fragment of local folk song in his *Lonely Waters*, hazy with the unique pearly light of the Broads. A folk song he brought from a more westerly part of the British Isles was an Irish piece, 'The White Mountain', which he treated in meditative style but which caught the public fancy in a brisker version sung by John MacCormack as *The Star of the County Down*. Another from the same source was the *Irish Love Song* he arranged in the 1920s. And in 1921 Moeran was again in East Anglia to take down some of the repertoire of the long-lived Harry Cox, born 1885, who was to contribute to the first gramophone record issued by the English Folk Dance and Song Society in 1932 and to play a seminal role in the post-war folk revival until his death in 1971.

While we are in Norfolk let us at least nod to a wraith even more insubstantial than Moeran's glimpse of *Whythorne's Shadow* or those shapes which wreathe across the waterways in late autumn and winter, and which itself drifted far from its home county. On 12th January 1239 the death of John Fornsete, a monk believed to have come from Forncett a few miles from Wymondham, was recorded in a monastic calendar at Reading Abbey. We know nothing about his personality, and certainly do not know why a piece of music, either composed or copied by Fornsete, should have been bound up in this document unless as a last affectionate tribute from his brethren. But the dating helps to establish the *Reading Rota* as the oldest authenticated canon, as distinct from plainsong and early attempts at harmonization. The manuscript is also the oldest to provide both sacred and secular words for the music – the more worldly alternative being known as *Sumer is icumen in*.

In 1751 an ambitious but resentful young organist and would-be composer arrived reluctantly in King's Lynn. Charles Burney, born in Shrewsbury on 7th April 1726, had been one of twins in his father's second marriage. The first Mrs

Burney had produced fifteen children, the second a mere five. The father would appear to have been a feckless type, flitting from job to job in an attempt to support his numerous offspring on sporadic earnings as a violinist and dancer. Charles's twin sister died when she was eight, by which time Charles and his elder brother Richard had already been sent to the village of Condover in the care of an elderly nurse. He attended school in Shrewsbury and then, when the family moved, in Chester. As choirboy and stand-in for the cathedral's gouty organist, he soon showed a flair for music both in theory and in practice. When the mighty Dr Arne stopped in Chester on his way back from Dublin to take up the position of composer at the Drury Lane Theatre, he was shown some of Charles's pieces, and was so impressed that he took the young man with him to London on a seven-year apprenticeship.

Charles was introduced to Handel and was soon playing in the orchestra for two new oratorios, *Hercules* and *Belshazzar*. It was wonderful experience, though all payments for this and other engagements went straight to Dr Arne. Then Burney came to the notice of Fulke Greville, who had a reputation for loose living but also a keen appreciation of the arts. Greville was keen to acquire Burney as household musician, and arranged a temporary lease from Arne, so that the young man found himself playing for his new host and guests in Greville's spacious country house at Wilbury near Andover. When Greville eloped, Charles Burney gave the bride away at a clandestine marriage, and was on such good terms with both of them that Greville decided to buy Arne out completely. When this had been done he wanted to take his new employee with them on a continental trip, only to find that Charles had fallen in love and was pleading for permission to marry. Greville generously released him from further obligations. Burney got a job as organist at St Dionis Backchurch and settled with his wife and daughter – born, as later researchers were to establish, a month before the marriage – into a house in Fenchurch Street.

Then the blow fell. Burney had been engaged to compose music for some of David Garrick's productions, and was directing a series of fashionable concerts in the King's Arms tavern, enjoying the company of men of wit and talent; but he was now overtaken by a mysterious fever. His doctor could not diagnose the real cause but was sure that the patient ought to leave London and reside in the country. Through influential personal contacts the MP for King's Lynn, Sir John Turner, arranged for Burney to be offered the post of organist at St Margaret's, the usual salary being increased on the understanding that he would teach music to children of the local gentry.

It was a terrible comedown. Conditions and musical standards of this provincial outpost were not to his taste:

> The Organ is Execrably bad . . . & the Ignorance of My Auditors
> must totally extinguish the few Sparks of Genius for Composition I
> may have, & entirely Discourage Practice, for Wherein wou'd any
> pains I May take to Execute a Meritorious tho' Difficult Piece of
> Music be repaid if like Orpheus I am to perform to Stocks & Trees.

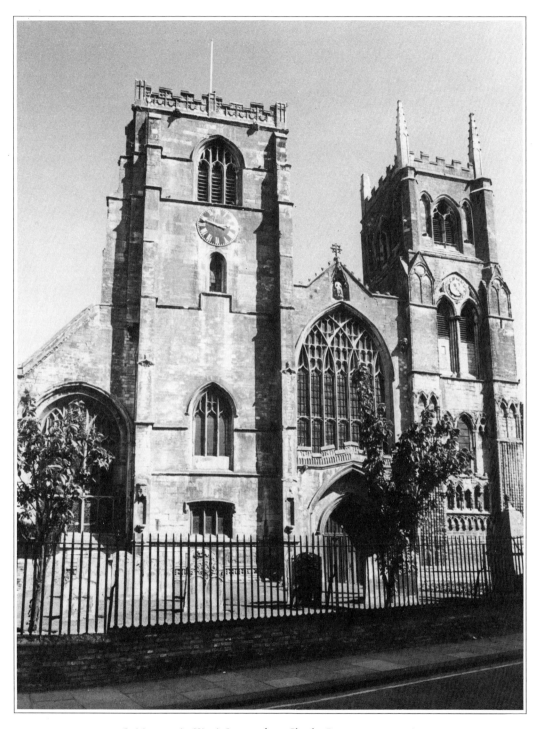

St Margaret's, King's Lynn, where Charles Burney was organist
between 1751 and 1755.

Then he began to adjust himself and make new friends. He managed to have a fine new organ installed in place of the decrepit old instrument. Also, with fewer distractions than London offered, he had time to study. He built up a library and was drawn more and more to the history of music, to which he was later to make a more famous contribution than ever he did with his own compositions.

Still he longed for success as a composer, and by 1755 was beginning to realize that this was unattainable unless he returned to the battlegrounds of London. It was a risky step. He needed a steady income, having by now six children to support. Nevertheless he gave in his notice at St Margaret's, and then was persuaded to stay on by an increase in salary. Only after further doubts and delays did he head back towards London in early 1760, setting up house in Poland Street. In 1767 the Burneys were briefly in King's Lynn again on family business, but Charles was soon to be off on continental travels in preparation for the *History of Music* which was to occupy so many of his subsequent working years in London, where for the time being we may well leave him.

From Diss in Norfolk a great madrigalist crossed the borders into Suffolk and then Essex. Born in 1574, John Wilbye was the third son of a tanner who must have had some musical interests since his will specified that John should have his lute. In his teens the young Wilbye was taken on as a musician in the household of Sir Thomas Kytson of Hengrave Hall, a few miles north-west of Bury St Edmunds. He made no attempt to seek greater rewards from other employers or to chance his fortune in London, but remained with the family for more than thirty years.

Hengrave Hall still stands in spacious parkland, close to its fifteenth-century church with a round tower of Saxon origin. The Tudor manor was constructed not from the familiar red brick of the time but from white brick and stone. In the Kytsons' day it had a moat, of which only a small segment remains. Between two towers the entrance is surmounted by a triple bay window with Renaissance putti and carved shields, including the arms of the Fishmongers' Company.

Since 1952 the building has been used as a convent school for girls, from whose Mother Superior permission must be obtained in advance by those wishing to see the interior with its Tudor fireplaces, lavish panelling, glass-painted scenes from the Creation to the Crucifixion, and the minstrels' gallery from which Wilbye and fellow singers and instrumentalists must often have serenaded their employers. Records have been preserved giving details of the household's musical resources and the furnishings of individual rooms, including Wilbye's room overlooking the church.

Sir Thomas also had a town residence in Austin Friars and it was from there that Wilbye, accompanying the family on their London visits, issued his *First Set of Madrigals* in 1598. Another volume appeared in 1609. He was a master of varying styles, from the sprightliness of *Ye that do live in pleasures plenty* to his preferred mood of dark emotion as in *Unkind, O stay thy flying* – music in which popular interest lapsed until its beauties, and those of many contemporaries, were brought to life again in this century, first by Charles Kennedy Scott with the publication of his Euterpe Edition of English Madrigals and the performances of

The gateway to Hengrave Hall, Suffolk, home of the Kytson family and their
household musician, John Wilbye.

the Oriana Madrigal Society under his direction, and, closer to our own day, by the incomparable counter-tenor Alfred Deller, his vocal consort, and his disciples and successors.

After Sir Thomas's death Lady Kytson remained in residence at Hengrave until her own death twenty years later. In 1613 she had given her resident musician the lease on what was accounted to be the best sheep farm in the neighbourhood. It must have occupied much of his time and attention, for although he continued to supervise music at the hall, he produced hardly any further work of his own.

When Lady Kytson died in 1626 her youngest daughter took Wilbye into her own household, which was none too happy a one. Life with her husband, Lord Rivers, at St Osyth grew less and less tolerable, until she left the estate in favour of the imposing brick mansion which still stands near the west end of Holy Trinity church, Colchester. Wilbye spent his last years here, died in 1638, and was buried at Holy Trinity, leaving his best viol to the Prince of Wales who was to become King Charles II.

The county of Essex offered a welcome to a composer of this century when, in 1913, Gustav Holst set out on a five-day walking tour. He found himself in Thaxted, which so pleased him that he soon took an old cottage in the hamlet of Monk Street, a mile or so south of the town on the road to Great Dunmow. The whole atmosphere was congenial, and he worked with a will not just for himself but for the local community. Conrad Noel, the provocatively Socialist vicar of the church with a taste for medieval music, had coached his choir in the half-forgotten lore of plainsong, and was now glad of Holst's help in reviving such forms.

In 1914 Holst began work on 'Mars', the first episode of his suite derived from the astrological attributes of *The Planets*, and had evolved a detailed outline just before the outbreak of the First World War. When this conflict started there were some local people only too ready to mumble suspicions about a man with such a foreign name, and information was laid against him as a spy. The police investigated but, not surprisingly, found no evidence.

Gustav Holst had in fact been born in November 1874 at 4 Clarence Road, Cheltenham, where today there is a small museum to his memory. His father, of Swedish extraction, had been a music teacher, his mother a pianist; and when Gustav went to the RCM it was taken for granted that he would concentrate on the piano. Instead he favoured composition, and, since severe neuritis made it impossible for him to attain any great proficiency at the keyboard, he took up the trombone and later played with the Carl Rosa Opera Company and in other orchestras. He was steeped in English folk music after researches shared with his close friend Vaughan Williams and with Cecil Sharp. It was an interest his daughter Imogen was also to share, doing much valuable work in her own right.

For much of his life Holst was to be employed in London, but made repeated forays into the countryside – whence *A Somerset Rhapsody* and *Egdon Heath* – and had an ear always alert for a genuine, rural turn of phrase in speech or melody. The undulating fields of Essex and the snug little hamlets were greatly to his taste, and Thaxted itself was all that an historic market town ought to be.

Thaxted church. While living in the town Gustav Holst set the words
'I vow to thee, my country' to a tune he called simply *Thaxted*.

Clusters of colour-washed, gabled cottages mingled with dignified merchant houses from the prosperous days of the wool and cutlery trades, all dominated by the Cutlers' Guildhall and the soaring spire of the largely fifteenth-century church with its pinnacles, gargoyles and buttresses.

On the Saturday and Sunday of Whitsun 1916 Holst brought singers and instrumentalists from St Paul's Girls' School and Morley College to augment the church choir in a festival of music by Palestrina, Bach and Purcell. This was followed on the Monday by folk songs and morris dancing. The Thaxted morris dancers still hold an annual festival in June and tour the region at Easter and on the Spring bank holiday.

That first Whit Sunday, the composer went into the mighty church between services and found he was not alone. A woman sauntering down the aisle was intoning a song without words and accompanying herself on the open strings of a violin. The eerie sound triggered off the idea for Holst's settings of medieval religious poems in *Four Songs for Voice and Violin*.

Another festival was held the following year and a third in 1918, by which time Holst had moved with his wife and daughter into the centre of Thaxted, where they lived in Town Street at The Steps (now called The Manse, with a plaque on the outer wall of the music-room) until 1925. A feature of the 1918 festival was a carol based on old verses found by the vicar, beginning as *This have I done for my true love* but always referred to by Holst himself as *The Dancing Day*. Dedicated to Conrad Noel, it also appears in an inscription on one of the church bells: 'I ring for the General Dance.'

Ordered to rest after a bout of overwork, Holst spent all of 1924 in Thaxted, writing his Choral Symphony, and then was back in harness in London. When he died in May 1934, just after sending greetings to the Whitsuntide singers at their festival in Bosham, his ashes were buried in Chichester Cathedral and the singers came to offer *The Dancing Day* in a last loving tribute.

In the year of Holst taking up his post at St Paul's Girls' School, another major English composer came into the world. Born in London on 2nd January 1905, Michael Tippett did not stay there long. His parents moved to Wetherden, a Suffolk village a few miles north-west of Stowmarket. The boy showed early signs of an interest in music and has since said that he was always positive he wanted to be a composer, though with little idea of what this might involve. He had private schooling at home and went to the village of Woolpit for Latin lessons. Knowing the vein of Celtic mysticism inherited from his Cornish father which was to infuse his later work, one cannot help wondering if he ever heard the story of the weird green-skinned children who were found centuries ago near a wolf-pit which gave Woolpit its name. They claimed to have strayed from a twilit fairyland beyond a broad river. One of them, a boy, soon died, but the girl lived on and married a man from King's Lynn.

In 1919 the Wetherden house was sold, and Mr and Mrs Tippett went to live abroad. At the age of seventeen their son went to his first symphony concert, conducted by Malcolm Sargent, and his old ambitions revived. He had difficulty in persuading his mother and father to let him study music full-time, but when

Michael Tippett's childhood home at Wetherden, with the barn in which he
and his brother played, and the sixteenth-century house to which his
father added an extension with a Rubens plaque in one wall.

they gave in he began studying composition at the RCM. Leaving in 1928, he
looked for work not in London but in the countryside. He settled into a cottage
near Oxted in Surrey, took up part-time teaching in nearby Limpsfield, and
helped in producing small-scale operas at the Barn Theatre, Oxted.

Not only was his musical style developing but also his political outlook.
Dismayed by the miseries of the slump and the hopelessness of the unemployed,
for a short time he became a Communist but soon found their ideas too rigid and
unproductive. His idealism, though, still led him to help many workers'
associations. He conducted an orchestra of unemployed musicians at Morley
College for Working Men and Women, and in 1940 became musical director
there, a post once held by Gustav Holst. At the outbreak of war his orchestra had
been supplemented by an influx of European refugees, and the effect of
persecution in Europe led him to work on a moving, deeply-felt oratorio, *A Child
of our Time*, which took two years to finish. It uses negro spirituals instead of
chorales, and many folk song elements in solo passages, and preached, in the
middle of war, pacifism as the only answer.

Tippett's stand as a conscientious objector earned him a three-month prison
sentence in spite of a personal intervention by Vaughan Williams. Released, he
continued working at Morley College. In March 1944 *A Child of our Time* was
first performed at the Adelphi theatre, with his friend Peter Pears as tenor soloist.

After the war the countryside lured him back, and in 1950 he moved into

Tidebrook Manor near Wadhurst in Sussex. Ten years later he moved again, this time to an old house near Corsham in Wiltshire; and finally to a modern house only a few miles away. In 1965 he became a frequent conductor with the Leicestershire Schools Symphony Orchestra and for them and local school choirs wrote *The Shires Suite*, invigoratingly led into by his treatment of the canon *Sumer is icumen in*.

Although still living this side of the river Tamar, Tippett remains a Celt by temperament, and has been heard to say that when travelling by train he can, even with his eyes shut, tell the exact moment when his compartment crosses the Cornish border. Certainly many of his preoccupations seem to stem from that ancient corner of Britain: his opera *The Midsummer Marriage*, though telling a modern tale of two couples undergoing very modern psychological ordeals, digs deep back into myth and ritual, and the very names of Mark, Jenifer and King Fisher remind us of Arthurian and other Celtic legends.

Tippett has come a long way from the Suffolk of his formative years, yet perhaps has never entirely escaped – not even into Cornwall. In his admirable short study of the composer, David Matthews points to one of the sections of the *Fantasia on a Theme of Corelli*, a pastoral andante, as evoking the horizons and whole atmosphere of the Suffolk rural landscape.

A younger composer who was also to become a conscientious objector in the Second World War also spent his youth in Suffolk but, unlike so many exiles, was to return to it during his most creative period.

Benjamin Britten was born on 22nd November 1913 – appropriately enough, St Celilia's Day, honouring the patron saint of music. His father was a dentist who liked music but disliked the gramophone or any other artificial means of disseminating it. He preferred listening to the real voices of his wife, secretary of the Lowestoft Choral Society, and her friends singing and playing. Young Benjamin, too, was delighted by the music, especially when professional soloists came to perform in Lowestoft and his mother put them up for the night.

The Britten children spent summer holidays on a farm near Butley. Here the Butley river runs across the marshes to join the Ore near what is now the bird sanctuary of Havergate Island, while behind the sumptuously carved stone frieze of heraldic shields on the ruined gate of Butley priory stretch the dark tracts of Rendlesham Forest and, of much older lineage, the twisted oaks of Staverton, a patch of primeval woodland almost untouched during or after the priory's possession of it. One can tread paths which offer a different note and a different breath every few steps: the East Anglian breeze never quite stilled, often rising to gale force; the crack of twigs underfoot or the plop of cones and branches deep in the wood; the call of wildfowl; and today, it must sadly be admitted, the sudden screech of military jets flying in low towards Woodbridge.

Sailing dinghies float like ruffled birds between Orford Ness and the mainland, scudding out from Orford or Slaughden near Aldeburgh. At Shingle Street the wind sings more piercingly, and the very name of the place warns one what scrunching, sliding sound to expect under one's shoes.

The first piece of contemporary music to attract Benjamin Britten's attention was Holst's *Song of the Ship-builders*, which he came across in a Lowestoft music shop. In 1924 he was taken to the Norwich Triennial Festival, where Frank Bridge was conducting his orchestral suite *The Sea*. The boy was overwhelmed, and when Bridge reappeared in Norwich three years later it was arranged that they should meet. At once they became firm friends, and young Benjamin spent several holidays with Bridge at Eastbourne or in London. When he went to Gresham's public school at Holt in Norfolk he had to combine work there with piano lessons from Harold Samuel in London and composition lessons from Frank Bridge at Eastbourne during the holidays. Britten was later to recall how Bridge would take him out on drives around Sussex, opening his eyes to the beauties of the little Downland villages and the churches of the region.

At sixteen Britten won an open scholarship for composition at the RCM, and on Bridge's suggestion studied under John Ireland. One of his first works of major importance was an affectionate tribute to the man who had done so much for him, *Variations on a Theme by Frank Bridge*.

Earning a living as a musician in the depressed 1930s was not easy. Britten wrote incidental music for films and the theatre, and collections of songs for schools. He had a stroke of good fortune in attracting the notice of the publisher Ralph Hawkes, who offered a contract for anything he produced. Towards the end of the decade he was able to buy an abandoned windmill at Snape and have it restored.

In 1939 he was in America giving recitals with Peter Pears when war broke out in Europe. Their mutual friend W. H. Auden had decided to become an American citizen, wanting no part of the Old World's troubles. Himself a pacifist, Britten was nevertheless unwilling to surrender his nationality. He and Pears went on working, though in increasingly homesick mood. One day Britten came across a copy of the BBC publication, *The Listener*, and read the text of a broadcast talk by E. M. Forster on George Crabbe. It conjured up so vivid a picture of the scenery around Aldeburgh that Britten felt he must return to it at once. While waiting for a berth on a homeward-bound ship he got his hands on a copy of Crabbe's poems and read 'The Borough'. Out of the dour tale of a surly, malicious community stepped the dramatic figure of Peter Grimes:

> He wanted some obedient boy to stand
> And bear the blow of his outrageous hand;
> And hoped to find in some propitious hour
> A feeling creature subject to his power.

On their return to their native country Britten and Pears had to appear before a tribunal as conscientious objectors. They were, however, allowed to tour and give recitals all over the country, and Britten worked on what was to become the *Serenade for tenor, horn and strings*. Whenever possible he returned to Snape, where his sister was looking after the mill, and in that congenial atmosphere walked and pondered and shaped the opera *Peter Grimes*, which was finished early in 1945 and first performed at Sadler's Wells on 7th June that year, with Peter Pears as the brutish yet tragic fisherman. The set and costume designer

'There is no sea like the Aldeburgh sea,' said Edward Fitzgerald.
'It talks to me.' It talked also to Benjamin Britten, who interpreted
its voice for the benefit of audiences worldwide.

stayed at Snape and breathed in the same atmosphere, basing many of the costumes on old Aldeburgh picture postcards.

The story is of an Aldeburgh 'native, rooted here' who has acquired an evil reputation in the Borough for his maltreatment of boy apprentices. Britten opens his opera with an inquest on a recent victim, and suggests wonderfully the mutterings of gossipy women in the background. In spite of warnings against ever employing a lad again, Grimes takes on a new apprentice whose safety is vouched for by the schoolmistress Ellen Orford, whom in gentler moments Grimes hopes to marry. On a Sunday when the boy ought to be allowed to rest, his taskmaster insists on their going out fishing, and the congregation note that he shows signs of bruises which suggest that 'Grimes is at his exercise' once more. The apprentice is in fact lost at sea, and when Grimes shows himself again in Aldeburgh the townsfolk close in on him. He takes his boat out to sea again alone and sinks it, and the tragedy ends with the locals singing fatalistically of a life forever governed by the moods of the sea, slaving on despite what disasters may befall.

Britten's skittish third opera, *Albert Herring*, derives from a Guy de Maupassant short story, but references to Iken and Snape make its basic Suffolk setting quite clear.

In 1947 Peter Pears suggested that instead of the English Opera Group grappling with expensive tours, they should mount 'a modest festival with a few concerts given by friends'. Why not, in fact, try an Aldeburgh Festival? It was decided to start in 1948 if the resources of the town's somewhat cramped Jubilee Hall proved manageable. Britten set to work on *Let's Make an Opera* with the restrictions of the hall in mind. The participatory nature of this work made it an instant success. The whole idea of this intimate yet first-rate Festival attracted so many music-lovers that before long it could be said of Aldeburgh, as Crabbe had said in his day:

> Soon as the season comes, and crowds arrive,
> To their superior rooms the wealthy drive.
> Others look round for lodging snug and small,
> The brick-floored parlour which the butcher lets ...

Local hotels and boarding-houses might manage to cope with visitors, but a regular Festival of any calibre could not forever be accommodated within the confines of that hall. Concerts and recitals spread out to enrich the countryside: choirs sang in Orford church, coaches delivered audiences to Framlingham and Southwold, and pianists played in the great church at Blythburgh, near the home of the composer William Alwyn, with wide-ranging views over estuary and heath. Still a worthier focus was needed for the main programmes. Britten and his colleagues turned their attention to his own village of Snape.

Here beside the river Alde stood a cluster of attractive brick buildings put up by the nineteenth-century engineering entrepreneur and iron-founder Newson Garrett. After prospering as a brewer in London, Garrett had begun malting at Snape at the highest navigable point of the river, using local barley and shipping

The Maltings at Snape, converted into a concert hall.

the finished product on a regular barge service to London. The Maltings expanded; the wharf was continually busy. By 1861 Garrett was reputed to own half the craft registered at Aldeburgh. His daughter, as hard-working and determined as himself, became the first woman doctor in England and, in 1908, the first lady mayor in England – Mayor of Aldeburgh, naturally.

Adjoining the Maltings then as now, the Plough and Sail public house flourished. Bargemen would drop barley seeds into cracks in the tables and drip beer over them, so that by the time they were clearing the river mouth the publican would find shoots of barley springing up from the woodwork.

But soon modern technology and big business mergers spelt the doom of local malting and the barge traffic. By the 1960s the main premises were up for sale, though nobody could have envisaged who the buyers would ultimately be. In May 1966 the Aldeburgh Festival organizers signed a long lease, helped by a covenant from Decca records, who were to use the acoustically brilliant hall for major symphonic recordings. Grants came from the Gulbenkian Foundation and the Arts Council, together with some £80,000 in the form of private donations. The conversion of what was to be the concert hall without destroying its external character was included in the annual Civic Trust awards for distinguished architectural projects. In June 1967 Queen Elizabeth II opened the new concert hall.

On the opening night of the 1969 Aldeburgh Festival the interior was burnt out.

Many an impresario would have given up at this stage, but the scheduled programme went ahead. The Bishop of St Edmundsbury and Ipswich immediately offered unrestricted use of certain churches in the diocese, and a writer at one of the concerts said that he 'sensed in the audience a feeling of identification which went far beyond sympathy – a steely determination that the values for which the festival stands shall not, and will not, be lost'. These values were in fact speedily reinstated. Within twelve months the Maltings hall was rebuilt with yet further improvements, and Queen Elizabeth came again to Snape to reopen it to a jubilant accompaniment of *Music for a Royal Occasion*.

Still the subsidiary venues offer their own special pleasures. Another of Britten's works encouraging the participation of young people, *Noye's Fludde*, was first performed in Orford church during the 1958 Festival and later in Southwark Cathedral, and has been repeated many times since. His church parables, too, will be associated by most of us with that delightful Romanesque building in whose porch George Crabbe's father used to act as local schoolmaster, and where *Curlew River* was first heard, to be followed by *The Burning Fiery Furnace* and *The Prodigal Son*.

Raised to the peerage during what proved to be his terminal illness, through which he still strove to bring out the music within him craving expression, Benjamin Britten died in 1976. He is gone, but leaves no mere ghost. His distinctive voice has not been stilled: it has been added to the Suffolk air and the rustling of Suffolk reeds along that winding course of the Alde from Iken to Snape. As we tread the towpath or the heaths and marshes, or trudge over the Aldeburgh pebbles, those of us fortunate enough to live in the neighbourhood sing to ourselves his idiosyncratic interpretations of old tunes such as 'Polly Oliver' or 'A brisk young widow', and over and over again the Suffolk song 'The Foggy, Foggy Dew', exported years ago to America but still most at home here, as Britten was and is forever at home here.

Imogen Holst, who contributed so much to the running of successive Aldeburgh Festivals, would surely approve of her father, Gustav, bestowing the last benison:

> Music, being identical with heaven, isn't a thing of momentary thrills, or even hourly ones. It's a condition of eternity.

6
The Northern Drift

O tell her, Swallow, thou that knowest each,
That bright and fierce and fickle is the South,
And dark and true and tender is the North.
Alfred, Lord Tennyson

Composers born north of a line through, say, the Wash and Wolverhampton have usually shown a defeatist tendency to drift south and be sucked into the maw of London, there to be broken down by the capital's digestive juices into something bland and easily assimilated, indistinguishable from other ingredients. It is sad that Britain should be so overbalanced. The creative artist who tears up his roots is all too likely to lose those components of his local soil which gave him his individuality. But London has always been the centre to which the artist has had to go to achieve fame; and the south is not so much bright and fierce, in Tennyson's words, as cosy and fashionable. Few northern composers from above our notional line went on working near their birthplaces, and few born below that line ventured on northern themes for their works, save for a few who chose to go right out of England and on into Scotland.

William Sterndale Bennett, for example, was born in Sheffield; Eric Coates at Hucknall in Nottinghamshire; George Dyson, who became director of the RCM in 1937 and a knight in 1941, at Halifax; Delius in Bradford; Edward German in Whitchurch, Shropshire; and William Walton in Oldham, which in a 1981 television biography he recalled with unequivocal loathing. None of these ever returned to his home town to work or retire, and few have so far shown any sentimental wish to be buried there. Yet the northern counties surely offer as much in the way of magnificent landscape and historical vigour to inspire the musical visionary as does any other part of the realm.

One of the most dedicated and fastidious composers of the century was born in May 1905 at Haslingden in Lancashire, a cotton and engineering town near

OPPOSITE
All that remains of Trimdon Grange colliery, County Durham, where an
explosion in 1882 killed sixty-eight men and inspired Tommy Armstrong's
ballad of the disaster, written to help the widows and orphans, and still sung
today at many a local function and on a number of
Tyneside records.

Accrington. Alan Rawsthorne began training as a dentist and then turned to architecture, but music took hold of him and in 1925 he went to the Royal Manchester College of Music. Later he taught at Dartington Hall, and was much in demand as a pianist. Not until he was in his thirties did he really begin to concentrate on composition, his first two compositions to command critical attention both being sets of variations, a form which was never to lose its appeal to him: perhaps his early interest in architecture had some bearing on the poise and elegant structure of his music. The second, for orchestra, is called Symphonic Studies and, although Rawsthorne felt little sympathy for the folk song and dance movement, there is no lack of energetic dancing rhythms in the variation which follows the opening Maestoso, or in the concluding fugue. His First String Quartet, 1939, comprises a set of six variations on a theme: the First Piano Concerto of that same year, starting with a finely spun Capriccio, is soon immersed in variation form in the central Chaconne, each variation modulating at the end so that its successor strives a semitone higher. This quest for a key through chromatic harmonies and shifting tonalities has much in common with the approach of Carl Nielsen, to whose work Rawsthorne was one of the first to draw serious post-war attention in this country.

Among his closest colleagues, Alan Frank was to speak of Rawsthorne's 'quiet understatement' and 'hatred of pomposity', while Alun Hoddinott praised his 'individuality of language, economy of means ... subtlety and refinement of thought'. Rawsthorne's perfectionism led him to revise the piano concerto, so that it did not have its first performance until a 1942 Promenade Concert, by which time he was in the armed forces. After service with the Royal Artillery he was transferred to the Army Film Unit, which he found very enjoyable. It was during this spell that he was asked to write an overture for ENSA (Entertainments National Service Association), and produced the bustling *Street Corner*, whose title speaks for itself.

After John Ireland had turned down the idea of a contribution to the Festival of Britain in 1951, Alan Rawsthorne was commissioned to provide his Second Piano Concerto. In this and in his Second String Quartet of 1954 he moves towards more formal and much larger scale sonata treatment, and there is a more richly romantic element in themes and scoring. But still that love of variation form has not been discarded: the final movement of the concerto is a set of three variations with a coda.

Also in 1954, long before anyone thought of building a popular stage musical around T. S. Eliot's verses in *Old Possum's Book of Practical Cats*, Rawsthorne wrote *Practical Cats* for a children's concert at the Edinburgh Festival. His selection from the book was made according to his personal view of the most logical musical sequence, melodically and rhythmically. Against the sometimes sardonic, sometimes lyrical flow and brusque comments of the orchestra, a speaker recites the virtues and otherwise of the cat on whom all well-ordered households depend, the cat who drowses on the vicarage wall, the boastful Gus recalling his melodramatic performances as 'the fiend of the fell' ... and the swaggering cat about town, whose pretensions are underlined by good-

The 'placid and bland physiognomy' of Old Deuteronomy on the vicarage
wall, drowsily depicted by Alan Rawsthorne
in his *Practical Cats* suite.

humoured parodies of Elgar. The whole thing ends with a helter-skelter jig for the
Jellicle Cats at the Jellicle Ball, taking off from a snatch of 'Boys and girls come
out to play'.

Alan Rawsthorne died in 1971, leaving little music that was overtly pictorial.
He did, however, allow himself one scenic exploration. Affection for *The
Compleat Angler* led him to write a suite for piano duet, *The Creel*, though
whether he was inspired more by Izaak Walton's wanderings along the river Lea
and his love of the view from Amwell Hill, or by his equally happy times in
Dovedale, it is hard to tell. Perhaps during his youth in Lancashire Rawsthorne
had more opportunities of visiting and being enchanted by Dovedale.

Whenever I travel through that part of the world I think not of the household
musicians who may have served the rich lords of the Derbyshire Peak District, but
of a few diminutive railway stations which function no longer. I frequently use a
route from which signposts point to Ambergate, and some miles further on is
Miller's Dale. In 1846 work began on a railway line from Ambergate which
would link Stephenson's existing line between Derby and Chesterfield to Cheadle
on the edge of Manchester. Running through a lovely valley of the Peak, this was
extended to Buxton in 1860, then ultimately closed in July 1968. The hiss and
rumble of steam engines no longer bounces back from the limestone walls, but
there is one echo I still hear: the melancholy call, 'Miller's Dale for Tideswell',
from the delightful Michael Flanders and Donald Swann song, *The Slow Train*,
with its other haunting incantations of Chorlton-cum-Hardy and Chester-le-
Street, Tumby Woodside, and Selby to Goole – all lost.

Miller's Dale station, Derbyshire, where the Flanders and Swann *Slow Train* will stop no more.

Earlier ballads had often lamented the arrival of the railways rather than their demise. In 1852 there was a public holiday to celebrate the first train to run officially along the line between Stourbridge and Evesham, with ten thousand cheering people awaiting its arrival at Evesham. One local resident, though, was in no mood to cheer:

> An old woman peeping at the line
>   Said I wouldn't care a farthing,
> But they destroyed my cottage fine
>   And cut away my garden
> Where I so many years did dwell
>   Growing lots of cabbages and potatoes,
> But worst of all my daughter Nell
>   Went off with the navigators.

During his work on documentary films, the young Benjamin Britten provided music for *Night Mail*, in which he had not merely to supply a purely musical accompaniment to W. H. Auden's poem but, with no more than half a dozen instrumentalists, devise all the requisite sound effects.

Another tuneful little memory of past railway pleasures is found in a lament for 'Dear old Stalybridge Station' in Cheshire, performed by a north-country club and theatre group of the 1970s and 80s, the Fivepenny Piece. And while we are in Stalybridge, a plaque on what was once the New Market inn in Corporation Street recalls another popular singer: Jack Judge, while staying at the inn, wrote *It's a Long Way to Tipperary* and first performed it on 31st January 1912 in the Grand Theatre, which then faced the inn from the other side of the street.

Cheshire boasts the birthplaces of two composers of recent times: John Ireland, born at a house called Inglewood in Bowden, and Cyril Scott from Oxton. Among Ireland's tone poems for orchestra and piano there can be found no title associated with his miserable childhood in the region. Scott returned from studies in Germany to give recitals and piano lessons in Liverpool but, like others we have mentioned, soon set off for London to make his reputation as performer and composer.

Liverpool has long had a tradition of concert-going to rival that of Manchester, and even in a public house pays tribute to the patron saint of music: the huge Victorian mass of the Philharmonic Hotel across the road from the Philharmonic Hall in Hope Street includes among its ornate panelling, tiling and stained glass a window depicting St Cecilia with the motto 'Music is the universal language of mankind'. Elgar's *Pomp and Circumstance March No. 1* was dedicated to the Liverpool Orchestral Society and first played there on 19th October 1901. In February of the following year Elgar was invited to write an ode for the forthcoming coronation of Edward VII. He decided to use the trio from the march to accompany the words of 'Land of hope and glory', despite his good friend Jaeger's protest that the mixture sounded 'damn vulgar'. The results we know to this day – and to the last night of the annual Proms.

Hilaire Belloc's poem about kindly Sally of Halnaker ('Ha'nacker')
Mill was set to music by Peter Warlock and by Ivor Gurney.

The grounds of Cliveden, where Arne's *Rule, Britannia*! was first performed.

The Mull of Kintyre, a far cry from Penny Lane in Liverpool, gave
rise to a Paul McCartney song released in November 1977
which became the first 'single' disc
to pass sales of two million in the United Kingdom.

The seeker after curiosities cannot help but be provoked by Vivaldi's 'Manchester Sonatas'. Do we dare conceive of a hitherto unrecorded visit by the Red Priest to make music in that city long before the days of the Hallé Orchestra? Alas: Vivaldi never set foot in England, and the group of sonatas is so named simply because the parts were found in a Manchester library.

In 1850 a German immigrant, Julius Delius, had settled in Bradford, Yorkshire, with the intention of enriching himself in the wool trade. He became a British citizen, and five years later married a German wife. He did indeed prosper so well that he was able to buy a house in Claremont, a private road off Horton Lane, out of Bradford and on the edge of the moors. Here were brought up fourteen children, of whom two died in infancy, and here the family entertained themselves with private musical evenings. Also, Julius Delius served on the management committee of the Hallé concerts, inaugurated by the German conductor Charles Hallé in Manchester but with regular performances in Bradford as well. So that the family could have a change of air from time to time, Julius took a furnished house at Ilkley. Here his son Frederick, born on 29th January 1862, loved to ride across Rumbold's Moor on a pony pretending to be a highwayman.

Although making no great mark at school, Frederick showed an intuitive talent for improvising at the piano. He took violin lessons from a member of the Hallé Orchestra brought over from Manchester for his benefit, but about the age of thirty abandoned the instrument and was never known to touch it again.

Fond as Julius was of music, he had no intention of allowing any of his children to contemplate a professional career. At eighteen Frederick was expected to join the family business. Sent to Germany to establish profitable contacts, he spent most of his time at the opera and in concert halls. The same thing happened during trips to Scandinavia and France, and when he went illicitly to Monte Carlo and won at the tables he spent his winnings on more concerts and violin lessons.

In clashes between father and son, Julius was adamant that Frederick should never regard music as anything but a domestic, amateur entertainment. At twenty-one, however, the young man's detestation of the wool trade became so obvious that his father backed him in a very odd venture, sending him to Florida in the belief that somehow he could make a success of growing oranges there. This line of business soon proved no more palatable than the one he had quit, but, in virtual solitude in a little wooden house on his estate, Frederick Delius was able to meditate for days on end about music. He bought a piano and made friends with a Catholic church organist some three days' journey away. This man, Thomas Ward, came to stay, and in six months gave Delius all the real academic training he ever had. Another visitor was Frederick's brother Ernest, to whom Frederick impulsively handed over the plantation while he went off to set up as a music teacher of fashionable young belles in Danville, Virginia. He was already developing his own style and harmonic idiom, but still craved the chance of studying further in Europe. This chance was offered only after Julius, having no notion where his son could have got to, sent a private detective on his trail with the promise that lessons in Leipzig would be paid for – for eighteen months only.

When Julius attempted at the end of that time to recall his son into the family business he was visited by Grieg, whom Frederick had met during a holiday in Norway. The famous composer spoke so warmly of the younger man's talents that Julius grudgingly continued his financial support, though this now dwindled to a mere pittance. After a while Delius went to stay with an uncle in Paris and there met Jelka Rosen, a Danish painter, who was to become his wife. He composed his first opera, *Irmelin*, and a number of other pieces; but nobody was interested in performing them.

Visits to England were few and far between. While staying with his sister at Folly Hall, Wibsey, he showed a reawakened interest in horses and enjoyed the local horse fair. Some boyhood memories stirred: he liked to stride across the moors, had a particular affection for Skipton Castle, and at one stage was so much taken by the 'Wuthering Heights' country that he planned a musical treatment of the Brontë novel – whether an opera or tone poem we shall never know, since he did not go ahead with the idea.

The first concert of Delius's works in his own country was at St James's Hall, London, in 1899. It featured some Danish songs, excerpts from an opera inspired by his American experiences, *Koanga*, and a symphonic poem for orchestra, *The Dance Goes On*, which was later revised as *Life's Dance*.

Shortly after this concert he was able to settle with Jelka in a house and grounds by the village of Grez-sur-Loing near Fontainebleau, which was to be his home until his death thirty-five years later. He loved France, yet must have felt some tug towards England, for the surroundings he had chosen were far from alien. Robert Louis Stevenson in one of his essays refers to the river bank nearby and 'a reach of English-looking plain, set thickly with willows and poplars'.

In 1907 a concert in the Queen's Hall first introduced an appreciative listener to the music of Delius. Thomas Beecham became a great admirer and, along with Peter Warlock, a most ardent proselytizer. In that same hall twenty-two years later Beecham organized and conducted a six-day festival devoted entirely to the composer's work.

When presented with the freedom of Bradford in 1932 – by special dispensation at his home in Grez, since he was too ill to travel to England – Delius said: 'I owe a great deal to Yorkshire. In my music much of my inspiration has come from the moors. I hope to get one more whiff of them before I die.' His hope was not fulfilled. He died at Grez on 10th June 1934, a few months after Elgar's death and a couple of weeks after Holst's.

Delius had expressed a wish to be buried in England in 'a churchyard that is very old'. To everyone's surprise his widow's choice fell on St Peter's, Limpsfield, in Surrey, a part of the world with which he had no known connection. Folk in Bradford were somewhat offended, but the council did send a wreath of heather and other Yorkshire moorland plants to the funeral ceremony at Grez. The body was brought for reinterment at Limpsfield on 26th May 1935. Jelka Delius, who had accompanied it to England, died of pneumonia two days later and was buried in the same grave.

A Yorkshire drystone wall in Delius's favourite walking and riding country.

Frederick Delius's self-taught style – not to say mannerisms – did not appeal to all his contemporaries. Vaughan Williams said that he sounded 'like a curate improvising'. Cecil Gray referred disapprovingly to his penchant for interminable sequences of chromatically descending sevenths; to which one might add his tendency to fall into lilting, lolloping nine-eight time. In spite of such criticism, Gray was one of the readiest to admit the spell which Delius could cast in a work such as *Brigg Fair*, when the countryside wakes on a summer morning with 'a faint mist veiling the horizon, and the fragrant scent of dawn in the air'. This conjuring up of a landscape is difficult to analyse. Of Dutch and German ancestry, married to a Danish wife, Delius claimed to prefer Nordic to English themes and atmospheres, and apart from that one spell in Florida spent most of his life in France. Yet from that home at Grez he wrote music which seems most wistfully true to the land of his birth. Even in such a supposedly classical form as a string quartet he could not help being pictorial, and the third movement of one of his two quartets is entitled 'Late Swallows'.

Percy Grainger once commented that Delius was not a man who cared to collect folk music 'in the field' and would not even appreciate a folk song unless it came to him already harmonized. The version of *Brigg Fair* which Grainger

Fields near Brigg, immortalized in *Brigg Fair*.

handed over was an arrangement for tenor and chorus. Once he had acquired it, Delius used the theme not so much as a basis for harmonic and contrapuntal variations as for characteristically rhapsodical musings.

When Delius grumbled in 1910 that his works were unfairly neglected, Grainger expressed the opinion that too many of them called for over-large forces and suggested he should try his hand at shorter pieces for smaller orchestra. Delius then produced *On Hearing the First Cuckoo in Spring* and *Summer Night on the River*. For all the drowsily English sound of the first, it was in fact founded on a Norwegian folk song already arranged by Grieg; and the wordless *Song of the High Hills*, which might suggest the Pennines, was another rhapsody inspired by Norway.

Recollections of the composer's youth in Yorkshire are enshrined, however, in his unusually austere yet loving *North Country Sketches*. The first of these portrays 'Autumn', with the wind sighing through the branches. Eric Fenby, the composer's musical amanuensis in his closing years, suggests that what we hear is the spirit of the wind rather than the wind itself, mourning the fall of the year and man's being shaken down just as leaves are shaken down. The 'Winter Landscape' which takes over is bare and hard, but the music maintains a secret, slow-breathing life below the surface. There follow a dance and then the 'March of Spring'. This last section was originally called 'Spring's Awakening', a more suitable title since there is no pretence of sustaining a marching rhythm throughout its entire length. Surging, burgeoning passages are broken by pastoral arabesques for oboe incongruously reminiscent of Smetana's depiction of lush Bohemian countryside in *Ma Vlast*. At the end, the march owes more to folk song than to military progress and here and there has an oddly Scottish snap to it.

A warmer work, *A Song of Summer*, was assembled with the aid of the devoted Fenby when Delius had become blind and paralysed. The composer painfully dictated a rearrangement of old material combined with some new fragments, telling his helper that he must imagine sitting on heathery cliffs, looking out to sea: the sustained string chords had to suggest the stillness of sea and land, and the clear sky over all. The piece was gratefully dedicated to Peter Warlock, who since his teens had espoused the composer's cause in a largely unreceptive England.

When Warlock, in his earlier incarnation as Philip Heseltine, came across Delius's music while still at Eton, there were no opportunities of hearing full-scale performances of the orchestral works, so he set himself to transcribe some of them for piano solo or piano duet. *Brigg Fair* was one of his earliest attempts. When he got to know Delius personally he continued his labours on such transcriptions with renewed fervour so that, in the days before radio and the long-playing record had made access to music so easy, people might learn to appreciate the composer's true magnitude.

In 1915, when D. H. Lawrence was in one of his not infrequent rages against England and the English and was dreaming of the Utopian colony he wished to set up somewhere else – anywhere else – Warlock wrote to Delius suggesting that the orange plantation in Florida which still belonged to him might prove a suitable site for this new commune. Delius would not hear of it: the grove had been neglected for twenty years and must by that time be a wilderness.

From 1925 to 1928 Warlock lived in the pretty little village of Eynsford in Kent and there, of all places, seems to have conceived a passing interest in brass bands. Still striving on Delius's behalf, he made an arrangement for brass band of *On Hearing the First Cuckoo in Spring*, thenceforth known to all its executants as 'The Brass Cuckoo'.

Brass bands are an essential part of the musical life of northern England, growing up as one of the most rewarding relaxations in the mining and mill towns. Queensbury, near Delius's home town of Bradford, is known to have had a band by 1816, though for part of its life this appears to have been largely a reed ensemble. Not until the middle of the century did it acquire its unmistakable style and the name of the Black Dyke Mills Band. Cheap rail travel made competition between neighbouring places easy and opened up the chance of national contests further afield. In 1853 a series was started at Belle Vue, Manchester. In 1856 a battle of the brass was mounted in Hull Zoological Gardens, and four years later its organizer, Enderby Jackson, persuaded the managers of the Crystal Palace at Sydenham to inaugurate the festivals which went on until the great building was burnt out in 1936.

For a long time British composers were reluctant to experiment with the resources of a purely brass ensemble. Approaches came from bandmasters rather than the composers themselves. Elgar's *Severn Suite*, dedicated to George Bernard Shaw, was commissioned for the 1930 Crystal Palace festival – though Elgar thriftily re-scored it for full orchestra in time for the 1932 Worcester festival. The conductor Harry Mortimer, having complained to John Ireland that composers were too snobbish to consider writing for brass bands, commissioned from Ireland a suite for the 1931 Crystal Palace contest. Following Elgar's example, Ireland was soon to rescue material from this *Downland Suite* by adapting two movements first for piano and then for small orchestra.

In 1936 Arthur Bliss wrote another test piece for the same annual festival, entitled *Kenilworth*. Herbert Howells tried his hand with *Pageantry*. Edmund Rubbra's *Variations on 'The Shining River'*, composed for the Albert Hall championship in 1959 and since used as a test piece in other contests, was based on a little piano piece from some years earlier. Other composers have made a special name for themselves in this genre: Eric Ball, for instance, with his virtuoso *Tournament for Brass*, and especially Henry Geehl, who died in 1961 after many years teaching at Trinity College of Music and composing and arranging for brass, including works such as the three-movement *Thames Valley Suite* with its lively opening picture of a Thames Regatta.

William Walton, born in Oldham, hated the whole background of his childhood. Sent as a choirboy to Christ Church, Oxford, he was bullied by other boys because of his Lancashire accent but, thanks to the help of an observant tutor, was admitted to the University proper as the youngest undergraduate since Henry VIII. Taken up by the Sitwells and invited to join them on a stay in Italy, he experienced a dismal trip across France in the rain – 'Not Oldham again?' he thought dispiritedly – but reached and fell in love with Italy, where he later settled. While working on *Belshazzar's Feast* he was installed in the stables of Reston Hall, a Northamptonshire house inherited by Sacheverell Sitwell. Only years later could he be tempted to overcome his murky memories of Oldham and its surroundings and compose a piece for brass band.

The great tradition of brass and silver bands in the north is matched by its choral reputation. One associates the Huddersfield Choral Society as surely with *Belshazzar's Feast* as with its innumerable renditions of a gargantuan *Messiah*. But something else which was once just as important, and more intimately and locally so, was the church band and choir. It is mildly surprising that no composer, to the best of my knowledge, has attempted even a minor work or any kind of affectionate pastiche based on such groups and their music. We have already seen the effect of Thomas Hardy's writings on English composers, yet not one of them has paid the vaguest tribute to the joys of the Mellstock Quire – in itself the sub-title of Hardy's bucolic idyll, *Under the Greenwood Tree*. The instrumentalists who fiddled and blew away in the organ loft, or played in place of an organ which the community could not afford, often provided the only music which remote parishes ever heard. From the eighteenth century until well into the nineteenth, a small band was the custom rather than the exception, and Hardy wrote often, in prose and verse, about the players and their foibles.

In the church of Holy Trinity at Balsham in Cambridgeshire, a few instruments are preserved in a glass case by the south door. The band is known to have been functioning up to 1840, with a platform to itself at the east end of the north aisle. At East Leake in Nottinghamshire is to be found a shawm, an instrument with a wide bell looking like a long trumpet but actually a woodwind instrument with a hint of the bassoon in its timbre: it was used in the church gallery to supplement the bass part.

At Warnham in Sussex, near Shelley's birthplace, one of the church treasures is a violin taken from the hand of a dying man. He was Michael Turner, local cobbler, who for fifty years served as parish clerk and sexton, and led the church choir. No local festivity was complete without Michael and his fiddle. When he died, the lord of the manor wrote an affectionate piece of doggerel as his epitaph:

> His duty done, beneath this stone
> Old Michael lies at rest;
> His rustic rig, his song, his jig
> Were ever of the best.
>
> With nodding head the choir he led
> That none should start too soon;
> The second, too, he sang full true,
> His viol played the tune.
>
> And when at last his age had passed
> One hundred less eleven,
> With faithful cling to fiddle string
> He sang himself to heaven.

Instruments laid out in the music gallery of the admirable Castle Museum in York are accompanied by notes on similar local functionaries, though some of them seem to have needed to pass an endurance test before starting to perform. At Sheffield in 1790 there was 'a kind of box, hung in chains' before the west window into which singers and instrumentalists had to climb by means of a ladder and from which they then made 'as loud a noise as the heart would wish' high over the gallery. William Mason of York, publishing a number of essays on church music in 1795, referred to the accompaniment of hymns and anthems by:

> scolding Fiddles, squalling Hautboys, false-stopped Violoncellos,
> buzzing Bassoons; all ill-tuned and worse played upon, in place of an
> Organ, which, if they had one, they would probably wish to improve
> by such instrumental assistance.

Church bands were gradually displaced by barrel organs and harmoniums. On one occasion during service at Crayke, near York, the barrel organ refused to stop and had to be carted out and down the churchyard still doggedly churning out the 'Old Hundredth'.

One musical craftsman in York managed to resist the blandishments of London and make a name for himself in his own city. Thomas Haxby, born in 1729, became parish clerk of St Michael-le-Belfry just after his twenty-first birthday, held this position until his death in 1796, and was also a 'singing man' at the Minster. His father had been a carpenter, and Thomas obviously inherited some technical flair, for there are early records of his having repaired the Minster organ bellows and then of his carrying out more substantial repairs and tuning the instrument. On one occasion, in lieu of cash, he received two bottles of wine.

Haxby began to expand on his own account, opening a music shop whose original frontage is still identifiable in Blake Street by two drainpipe heads marked TH 1773, and manufacturing keyboard instruments. The Haxby spinet was much sought after, and Dr Arne is known to have possessed one. Orders were accepted for repairing or substantially rebuilding organs: Haxby improved the organ of Leeds parish church, and installed completely new ones in St Mary's at Scarborough and St James's at Louth. He also tendered for renovating the organ in Beverley Minster in 1767, but did not get the contract.

Beverley has a significant memento of its musical past. In the nave of St Mary's church is a pillar dating from the early sixteenth century with stone statuettes of minstrels on the capital and the inscription 'Thys pyllor made the meynstrels'. This musical offering seems to have been provided by those members of a guild 'playing of any musical instruments ... between the rivers of Trent and Tweed' who had the right to exclude and fine any strolling players not of their fraternity, and who met annually in Beverley to appoint officers and admit any brother worthy of the honour 'or else of some honesty and cunning' – which one assumes to mean skill rather than slyness.

At Ripon in the seventh century Bishop Wilfrid founded an abbey and there encouraged the practice of Gregorian chant. He also established the great abbey at Hexham in Northumberland, where the skill as cantor of Maban, a monk from Canterbury, is spoken of by Bede.

A few miles north of the city of Durham we can visit the home of a recluse whose memory provokes a number of queries in the minds of musicologists. Past a rubble of old army bunkers and derelict huts near Plawsworth, past rusty sagging fences and corrugated iron, there is a sharp descent into the valley of the river Wear, its waters rustling and sparkling in a tight loop over the rocks. A track leads bumpily through a busy farmyard to where, on the edge of the river, sheltered from winds by the steep bank opposite, is the mellow brown ruin of Finchale Priory. Northwest of the high altar is marked the grave of St Godric.

Godric was born in 1065, probably in Norfolk, and after a spell as a pedlar took to the sea. He would appear to have been something of a freebooter and has been associated with that 'Goderic, a pirate from the Kingdom of England' who escorted King Baldwin I of Jerusalem through an Egyptian blockade into Jaffa. But after his dubious experiences in the Crusades, Godric gave up the sea and adopted the life of a hermit, first near Carlisle and then in a cave in Weardale. Given permission by Bishop Flambard of Durham to make himself a hermitage at Finchale, he is said, in spite of his habit of standing in a hole in the river bed so that water came up to his neck, to have survived until the age of 105. After his canonization his tomb and chapel were incorporated in a Benedictine priory. During the sixty years at Finchale he wrote poems about his visions, also jotting down songs acquired on his travels in an odd combination of the secular and liturgical.

In Newcastle upon Tyne we find traces of that rare bird, the local composer who achieved fame in his own day but refused to be lured away to London. Charles Avison was baptized in St John's church on 16th February 1709, fifth child of Richard Avison, 'one of ye Waits'. After studies in Italy he returned to become, in July 1736, organist to the church of his baptism, but only a few months later was appointed to St Nicholas's, now Newcastle Cathedral.

Although Avison was to hold this post for more than thirty years and to be succeeded by his son Edward, his musical interests were by no means exclusively religious. Almost immediately after the appointment he organized the first public subscription concerts in the town, out of doors in summer and indoors in winter, first at the Assembly Room in the Groat Market and occasionally in the Turks Head Hotel, which was then in neighbouring Bigg Market. Similar functions were also arranged in Durham. On several occasions they were followed by dancing and card playing. It was not an invariable practice in those days to list the names of composers on programmes, but there is evidence that Avison introduced many new and important works to the public, including those of Handel, though he himself considered Geminiani far superior. He also featured some of his own compositions: admiring the Italian style, he adapted some of Scarlatti's keyboard pieces for string orchestra, and published fifty violin concertos of his own, plus a number of quartets and trios, and also sonatas for violin and harpsichord in the style of Rameau.

In John Wesley's Journal there is an entry for February 1765 praising the first

Finchale Priory, built around the shrine of St Godric.

The Newcastle church, now the city's cathedral, in which Charles Avison was
organist for more than thirty years: beside it, a sign points out the
road to Blaydon, where the races were held.

performance of *Ruth*, an oratorio filled with 'exquisite music' which 'might
possibly make an impression even upon rich and honourable sinners'. This work
fell into three parts, the first of which was composed by Avison, the second and
third by Felice de Giardini, who came from Italy to teach and play in London for
some thirty years. Someone upon whom it did not make a favourable impression
was Haydn, who heard it in Ranelagh Gardens, London, at a benefit performance
with the aged Giardini himself playing the violin – 'like a pig', said Haydn.

Avison himself resisted invitations to settle in London, where his name had
become respected as much for his critical and theoretical writings as for his actual
compositions. A century later his reputation still stood so high that a march in the
possession of Robert Browning's father prompted the poet to include Avison in
his *Parleyings with Certain People of Importance in their Day*. He died in May
1770, and is buried in St Andrew's beside his wife, who had predeceased him by
four years.

In the Cloth Market, running roughly parallel to the Groat Market from Bigg
Market, in which Avison had his assemblies and concerts, is another centre of
Tyneside music. Here, in what started out as the Wheat Sheaf Inn, a Royal
Promenade Music Saloon was open every evening for the entertainment of the
townsfolk, changing its name to Mr John Balmbra's Cloth Market Music Saloon

after Balmbra had taken the place over and set his imprint on it. In these premises, one evening in 1862, George Ridley first sang what was to become pretty well the national anthem of Tyneside.

Ridley was born in 1835, son of a man who struggled for a living sometimes as a ropemaker, sometimes as a pitman. Young George himself was put to work in a colliery when he was eight, but at eighteen switched to the job of waggonman in an ironworks. He got to know the Wheat Sheaf early on, winning the prize of a new hat as the best comic singer in an amateur contest there. In 1856, crushed under a waggon and so badly injured that he could find no steady work, he set out to scrape a few pence together by singing in local music halls and supper rooms. One of his venues was the Blaydon Mechanics Institution Lecture Hall for their 'Popular Fortnightly Music and Dramatic Entertainment'. He went on tour, but was soon glad to get back to the banks of the Tyne where his own lyrics and music sounded most at home.

It was in Balmbra's concert room that 'Geordie' Ridley first offered the public the saga of that 'ninth of Joon, eiteen hundred an' sixty two' when a happy crowd assembled at Balmbra's to take the bus 'alang the Scotswood Road, to see the Blaydon Races'. These races had begun the previous year and were held annually until 1916, when they had to be discontinued because of riotous behaviour. After his greatest success Ridley lived only another two years, suffering from the effects of his accident, but in that time wrote a number of memorable songs. The last one, *Cushie Butterfield*, not merely stole the tune of *Pretty Polly Perkins* but grotesquely parodied its sentiments, and resulted in Ridley having to leave town for a while: both the unappetizing heroine and her cousin, Tom Gray the muckman, were real people who took great exception to being caricatured.

Ridley died on 30th September 1864 and was buried at St Edmund's, Gateshead. But the music hall tradition he had done so much to strengthen did not die with him. Others tried to emulate him; others still pursued their own ways but acknowledged their debt to him. A singer inspired by Ridley was Joe Wilson, best remembered for his lyrics of *Keep your feet still, Geordie hinney* – the tune, like so many, having been stolen from another popular song. Wilson died at the age of thirty from tuberculosis. On his tombstone is carved:

> It's been me aim to hev a place i' the hearts of the Tyneside people,
> wi writin' bits o' hyemly songs aw think they'll sing.

Balmbra's is still there, on what is now a pleasant pedestrian precinct. Its vaulted concert room is a plushy delight, with velvety maroon wallpaper and the tables and benches of a true old-time music hall. Prints of Geordie Ridley garnish the bar. But on my last visit the hall was running a disco four nights a week, with folk groups on Wednesdays.

Earlier in the century Bobby Nunn, a blind fiddler, had sung and played in pubs and at social gatherings with topical verses often more scurrilous than those about Cushie Butterfield and Tom Gray. He added to his takings by promoting early 'commercials': one of his ditties was an advertisement for boot polish, whose manufacturers paid him half a crown for featuring it. In the year of

Blaydon Races he wrote a more serious song about the disaster at Hartley when 200 pitmen were buried alive, including boys of six and seven years old, and took it round the halls to boost funds for the widows and orphans. Mining tragedies and terrors were all too common a subject for grim ballads, some of them lit nevertheless with the wry humour and defiance of the men who worked the seams. The eighteenth-century *Collier's Rant* became what in modern radio parlance might be called the signature tune or theme song of the Northumbrian miners, and in July 1946 was sung by massed choirs at the ceremony of hoisting the Coal Board flag over the newly-nationalized pits.

The gruelling life of nineteenth-century pitmen became the subject of an opera by Alan Bush. Born in London on 22nd December 1900, Bush studied at the RAM, where he was later to become Professor of Composition, and in Berlin. By the middle thirties he was an avowed Communist, took over from Rutland Boughton as conductor of the London Labour Choral Union, and served as chairman of the Workers' Music Association. Although some of his works favour an English modal idiom, their driving force has always been as much social conviction as primarily musical expression, resulting in such cycles as *The Songs of the Doomed*, his first opera *Wat Tyler*, dealing with the Kentish rebellion, and his *Ballad of Aldermaston*. The opera was first produced in East Germany, as was his second, *Men of Blackmoor*. The libretto for this drama of Northumbrian miners was written by his wife after they had visited Newcastle upon Tyne in 1953 for purposes of research.

While they were in those parts Bush heard Jack Armstrong, outstanding virtuoso of the Northumbrian bagpipes or 'small pipes', and was so taken by their gentle chamber music quality that he composed *Three Northumbrian Impressions* for the instrument. The Prelude strikes one at first as a Bach pastiche but soon acquires its own character, though with a disconcerting resemblance to *Oh, will you wash my father's shirt*. The Lament is alternately impassioned and meditative, with trills and shakes like those of a fluent organ. The third dancing movement is based on an old Northumbrian pipe tune. Overall these small pipes, inflated by a bellows pumped by the arm instead of by a blow-pipe as in Scotland, offer greater possibilities of staccato playing, a gentler fluting timbre, a wider compass of notes, and less lingering discord than the larger Highland pipes. There is a fine collection, with a wealth of explanatory material, in the National Bagpipe Museum at the Black Gate, Newcastle.

I wish we had more opportunities of hearing Bush's *Nottingham Symphony* and also another of his essays on a local subject, *Trent's Broad Reaches*. Fortunately I did hear one morning recently his *Liverpool Overture*, composed in 1973 for the 125th anniversary of the Liverpool Trades Council. The occasion may sound a solemn one, but the overture is in fact a most engaging interweaving, not too dissimilar in purpose from Brahms's *Academic Festival Overture*, of maritime themes appropriate to the great port, graced by some sections of ebullient pastiche.

A composer in political sympathy with Alan Bush during work with choirs in the Depression years was the slightly younger Michael Tippett who, as we have

OPPOSITE, ABOVE
Every Shrove Tuesday the ducal piper, last of all English family pipers,
leads a procession from Alnwick town to the pastures below the castle where
an annual football match is played. The traditional Percy family pipe melody,
Chevy Chase, tells of a victory over the Scots in a somewhat muddled
mixture of the actual battles of Otterburn and Humbleton Hill.

OPPOSITE, BELOW
Trent's Broad Reaches at Nottingham, two sources of works by Alan Bush.

already noted, joined the Communist party but was soon disillusioned. In 1932, while still moving towards that brief commitment, he joined in a scheme to help men who had been put out of work by mine closures. These were not collieries but ironstone mines at Boosbeck in the Cleveland region of North Yorkshire. Work camps were established for the unemployed, and after a production of *The Beggar's Opera* Tippett composed a ballad opera of his own, *Robin Hood*, glorifying the heroic deeds of that famous defier of all oppressors and exploiters. It was performed at Boosbeck in 1933. Local miners were perhaps not too dismayed when 1939 came, for the workings were soon reopened to supply material for the war effort.

One Newcastle musician in particular will be remembered for his part in that war. He was the quirky, enthusiastic W. G. Whitaker, born in 1876, who trained and conducted college choirs in Newcastle, numbered among his compositions two with a local flavour – *A Lykewake Dirge* for chorus and orchestra, and *Among the Northumbrian Hills* for piano quintet – and died in July 1944 in the Orkneys after strenuous service as musical director of Scottish ENSA.

If it is odd that no composer should have captured the Mellstock Quire in music, it is surely downright amazing that none has been inspired by one of Britain's mightiest historical monuments in this northern land. From Wallsend-on-Tyne to Bowness-on-Solway stretches the awesome rampart of Hadrian's Wall, resonant with the history of the Roman occupation and later clashes, changing colour and mood and character from day to day, season to season. Yet there is no major tone poem, suite, song cycle or anything else to transform its ancient inner music into notes and chords.

7
Seascapes

I love the sailor of the waves
Who upon the fiddle plays,
On the Jew's harp, on the viol,
On hollow chanter of great pipe . . .
Hebridean song

The most celebrated account of the *Principall Navigations, Voiages and Discoveries of the English Nation* appeared in 1589. Its author, Richard Hakluyt, had learned several languages in order to interview sailors who came from all over the globe to visit him, but when revising and expanding his 'prose epic of the English nation' during the last sixteen years of his life he chose to make his headquarters not in a busy port but in the quiet rural village of Wetheringsett in Suffolk. Even there he remained obsessed by the glories of distant oceans and their great English navigators.

Thomas Arne, thoroughly cosmopolitan by nature, was nevertheless moved to conclude his masque *Alfred*, composed for a fête given at Cliveden by Frederick, Prince of Wales, in August 1740 with the first performance of a stirring xenophobic air entitled *Rule, Britannia!* And in many a pub and village hall far from the coast can still be heard, when people turn to singing old ballads rather than current favourites, the echoes of shanties and fishing songs, seafaring ditties of all kinds which still strike a chord in the hearts of a maritime nation. It is hardly surprising that each season of Promenade Concerts traditionally nears its close with Henry Wood's *Fantasia on British Sea Songs*, devised in 1905 as a centenary salute to Nelson's victory and death at Trafalgar.

The shanty was basically a work song, with a strong rhythm and repetitive phrases and choruses to ease the labour of heaving on capstan bars or other tasks where steady, concerted effort was needed. Some tell of distant places, as in 'Bound for the Rio Grande' and 'Shenandoah'; some are rollicking or practical celebrations of life on board, as in 'Haul the Bowline' and 'Blow the Man Down'; while 'Shallow Brown', a survivor from the days of sail before steam and oil did away with the need for 'hauling shanties', has a theme which recurs both in work songs and in less strenuous refrains – the lass on the quayside, sighing for her

OPPOSITE
'Sea Drift'

129

wandering sailor lad. Obvious complements were the wanderers' sung promises to remain true and come home one fine day.

E. J. Moeran found an attractive piece in Norfolk and arranged it as *The Sailor and Young Nancy*, in which the departing mariner vows that 'If ever I return again I will make you my bride'. Everyone knows of the optimistic Northumbrian girl whose Bobby Shafto will come back and marry her. Some did return and wed. Others were faithless; and there were those who failed to return through no fault of their own. Alex Glasgow frequently sings a sad little song, 'My Bonny Lad', in which a waiting girl is told that her sweetheart's 'grave is green, but not with grass' and that she should never lie beside him. One of Vaughan Williams's *Five English Folk Songs* is *The Lover's Ghost*, in which the phantom of a sailor comes to claim his true love.

John Ireland's setting of John Masefield's 'Sea Fever' must be one of the most frequently performed songs of this century, though such performances have all too often been given by inadequate baritones in pier pavilions or village halls. Its success has overshadowed another of his Masefield settings, *The Bells of San Marie*, which depicts a mythical afterworld for sailors where all they need ever do is spend dreamy days ringing leisurely carillons.

Percy Grainger adapted many maritime themes to his own purposes and gave a nautical flavour to others. *Molly on the Shore* combines two Irish reels which so attracted him that he scored the piece for string quartet, then small orchestra, then a large orchestra. Generous as ever to his friends, he provided Holst with the basis of *Swansea Town*.

The Fishermen of England is a fine, rousing piece, but there is a more authentic ring in the factual, almost documentary songs of fishermen around the British Isles. Old songs of that 'queen of the sea', the 'silver darling', the herring, still blend quite naturally into new songs on the same bleak yet captivating theme. It is clear from the lyrics that many songs were sung not merely about the fish but *to* the fish. Their pursuers plead with them, coax them: 'Come on, spin up, my darlings ...' And there is the great rejoicing when the 'heavin' an' haulin' an' shakin' the nets' brings 'a sheet of silver' in over the side.

Scots girls who used to travel down the Lincolnshire and East Anglian coasts to clean and barrel the herring left a legacy of cheeky songs with a Scottish lilt now mingling or clashing with local versions, and at times introducing a wistful note into recollections of those long-gone days of toil and flirtation along the Yarmouth quays.

Songs, like people, have a habit of wandering across boundaries and changing outlook. *Sailors for My Money* was written by Martin Parker around 1635 and issued as a street ballad or broadside. Its reproof to 'Countrie men of England, who live at home with ease' and give no heed to the seamen who must battle on 'how ere the wind doth blow' led on to a variant, *When the Stormy Winds do Blow*, which has lasted on into our own time, possibly helped on its way by Thomas Campbell's derivative parlour and end-of-pier favourite, *Ye Mariners of England*.

Sentiments were less buoyant in the 1920s and 1930s, when a glut of fish and a

The fishing fleet still remembers 'three score and ten, boys and men ... lost from Grimsby town' in a ballad of 1889 – as well as more up-to-date songs of social protest against the decline of the cod and herring fisheries.

national slump brought poverty and despair. Today the overfishing of the North Sea and the crippling of the herring fleets has left ports like Lowestoft and Fraserburgh in almost as desperate a plight, and driven contemporary singers to songs of social protest. It's a far cry from the confident days of one of the most popular composers and performers of the eighteenth century, who issued a stream of patriotic numbers in which he threatened that Britain would 'bang the Spaniards, belabour the Dutch, and block up and laugh at the French' – aggressive talk which would hardly endear us to the European Community today, but accorded well with the sentiments of his time.

Charles Dibdin was born in Southampton in March 1745 and christened in Holy Rood church, the sailors' church whose remains now form a Merchant Navy memorial. His grandfather is said to have founded the village of Dibden, overlooking Southampton Water. His father, a silversmith, was also parish clerk to Holy Rood, and Charles, the twelfth of fourteen children, was originally intended for a clerical career. Sent to Winchester, he became a junior chorister and soon showed an aptitude for music of all kinds, sang at local public concerts, and before the age of sixteen was brash enough to apply for the post of organist at Bishops Walton.

His favourite elder brother, Tom, soothed his hurt pride after rejection of the application by inviting Charles to join him in London for a while, where he tried the organs in various churches and was sometimes allowed to play the congregation out of St Bride's, Fleet Street – close to where that earlier composer, Weelkes, was buried.

Eager to make a name for himself, Charles seized the chance of working for a music publisher in Cheapside but spent most of his time composing songs and trying to persuade his employer to publish them. When his brother had sailed away in charge of a merchantman, leaving him to his own devices, he went direct to some of the leading singers in the various pleasure gardens and at last succeeded in having a few of his ballads performed at Finch's Grotto Gardens in Southwark. He was then encouraged to try his hand at a theatrical piece staged at the Theatre Royal, Covent Garden, and did so with remarkable success. The hit song of the show was one he had written when he was fourteen – *In every fertile valley*, a melody which, once heard, haunts the listener as exasperatingly as any modern jingle but with far more just cause. Dr Arne bestowed his blessing on the young upstart, and it looked as if Dibdin's future was assured. Under the management of the equally famous David Garrick he contributed to Theatre Royal productions, and in due course was appointed Exclusive Composer to Covent Garden.

While prospering in this direction, though, Charles was fomenting trouble elsewhere. He married, but left his wife to go and live with an actress who bore him two sons, Charles and Tom, named after his idolized brother. This adoration of brother Tom showed itself in a succession of nautical songs – some symbolic, as in *This life is like a troubled sea*, some sternly condemning the authorities for peacetime neglect of their gallant seamen, others rallying men to the cause and deriding all their enemies. Dibdin explained his motives:

> I conceived that . . . duty might assist inclination, and therefore as a
> prominent feature in my labours I sung those heroes who are the
> natural bulwark of their country. This theme which perhaps more
> from zeal than ability I have fortunately handled, had only been
> slightly touched upon until I undertook it; and, though we have had
> some poetic specimens of nautical praise, the character of the British
> tar plain, manly, honest, and patriotic, had not been very pointedly
> put forward.

At a time when Charles was in financial difficulties because of domestic problems
and his imperious quarrels with most of the London managements, Tom died at
sea, leaving him some money in India. Dibdin raised the cost of the fare by selling
off a number of his unpublished songs for a pittance and making a solo tour of the
country, during which progress he was twice asked by mayors of towns he was
visiting if he was quite sure his entertainment was perfectly proper and 'would
not corrupt the apprentice boys'. When he did at last set sail it was to find that the
reality of the sea was not as splendid as he had thought, and that British sailors
were not all sturdy and dependable: he endured a mutiny and a storm in the
Channel, and decided to quit the ship before it had left English waters.

In spite of setbacks he was buoyed up by a new *amour*, whom he was to marry
and celebrate as his 'lovely Nan' in many a song with lines such as 'My ship's
called the Nancy, and Nancy's my wife'. Gradually he struggled back to solvency.
From 1789 onwards his solo performances of song and comedy were increasingly
successful. When war broke out with France he redoubled his efforts in writing
sea songs, and it has been recorded that Napoleon considered Dibdin to have
done more for our naval glory than any of Nelson's achievements. When the fleet
mutinied at Spithead and then the Nore, Dibdin was officially despatched to sing
to the mutineers and restore their sense of patriotic duty.

There was a time when he felt bitterly that his endeavours had not been
sufficiently recognized:

> Have my sea-songs procured me a single public compliment from the
> navy? On the contrary . . . though in common with the rest of the
> world I have learnt that my songs have been considered as an object
> of national consequence; that they have been the solace of sailors in
> long voyages, in storms, in battle; and that they have been quoted in
> mutinies, to the restoration of order and discipline, all of which I
> could indubitably prove, if it were worth my while; yet the only
> symptom of acknowledgment I ever received, was a hearty shake by
> the hand from Admiral Gardner, when I gave him my vote for
> Westminster.

Acknowledgements were not, however, entirely lacking. William Pitt granted
Dibdin a pension of £200 a year in recognition of his services to the nation, and at
the age of sixty the composer retired, supplementing his income by the sale of
rights in over 300 of his 1,000 songs, among which were such lasting successes as

The Bells of Aberdovey. 'Pretty safely arrived in port,' he recorded with relief, 'tolerably well laden.' But he was incensed by those who pirated or plagiarized his songs, and even more incensed when a change of government resulted in the abrupt abolition of his pension. Returning to the task of making a living, he went into music publishing on his own account; and went bankrupt.

During this fraught period he somehow found the strength to write more music, among this one of his loveliest melodies, offering a toast to 'the wind that blows, the ship that goes, and the lass that loves a sailor'.

Outraged by official treachery, the public raised a subscription to help Dibdin and ultimately shamed the authorities into restoring the pension. He lived out his few remaining years with Nan and their daughter in Arlington Road, Camden Town, and was buried nearby in St Michael's churchyard, where his tombstone was engraved with the words from his most famous song, *Tom Bowling*, written in memory of his brother Tom:

> His form was of the manliest beauty,
> His heart was kind and soft.
> Faithful below, he did his duty
> And now he's gone aloft.

The grave of Charles Dibdin in St Martin's Gardens, off Camden Street in Camden Town.

The Grand Hotel, Eastbourne, where Debussy stayed while completing *La Mer*
and the first set of *Images*.

Loving his Nan and approving of all pretty lasses who loved sailors, one wonders what Dibdin would have made of the aggressively feminist Dame Ethel Smyth who, born in London in 1858, stoutly declared her allegiance in the suffragette anthem, *March of the Women* for chorus and orchestra. She, too, tackled a couple of nautical subjects: an opera, *The Wreckers*, which started with a French libretto and was first produced in Germany in 1906 before attaining a London performance at Her Majesty's Theatre in 1909; and a comic opera based on a W. W. Jacobs story, 'The Boatswain's Mate', which had its première on 28th January 1916 at the Shaftesbury Theatre. The overture of *The Wreckers* shows up occasionally in the concert hall, but little else of this ferociously earnest composer is likely to live as long as Charles Dibdin's artless yet unforgettable tunes.

Other British composers – not to mention visitors to these shores – have turned their gaze out over the great waters. Elgar's song cycle *Sea Pictures* was written for the 1899 Norwich festival and conducted by the composer. The five poems on which it is based (one of them written by Elgar's wife Alice) are of uneven quality, but there is no gainsaying the skill and passion of the first piece, 'Sea Slumber Song', where harp and strings and a somnolently reverberating gong convey the surge of long swells and deep troughs. In 1908 Delius's *Sea Drift*, the setting of a poem by Walt Whitman, already performed in Germany, made its first English appearance at the Sheffield festival. To another northern festival, that of 1910 in Leeds, came Vaughan Williams's *Sea Symphony* for soprano and baritone with chorus and orchestra. This is unashamedly 'programme music'. After an opening surge from B minor to bright D major, we hear the rise of a Whitman poem once again, the tumult of the deep, and hints of shanty tunes, until in the closing sections the injunction 'Steer for the deep waters only' does indeed steer us out on to a tranquil ocean. 'Behold the Sea', indeed: and how much more vivid it is than Arthur Somervell's later but more old-fashioned attempt at a similar feat in his Symphony in D, *Thalassa*, in 1913.

Eastbourne seems too cosy a place to generate much nautically musical passion, but two major works came ashore here, as it were. In the summer of 1905 Debussy was staying in Eastbourne after some troublesome times in his own country. He had left his wife, who tried to kill herself, in favour of a well-to-do businessman's wife, who presented him with a daughter and whom he later married. Spurned by his friends, he found the time and inspiration in Eastbourne to complete the three orchestral sketches which make up *La Mer*. Is it too fanciful to think one can see and hear in the central piece, 'Jeux de vagues', the shifting glimmer of the great expanse of water below Beachy Head?

One composer who loved to look out over those waves was Frank Bridge. Born at Brighton in 1879, he spent most of his creative life in Sussex and was to die at Eastbourne in 1941. On a scholarship to the RCM he studied alongside Vaughan Williams, Holst, and John Ireland. In his professional life he was in great demand as a viola player and as a conductor, being often called in to deputize for Henry Wood. His first great public impact as a composer was with an orchestral suite, *The Sea*, in 1912. Its four movements are 'Seascape', 'Sea-foam', 'Moonlight', and 'Storm'. A performance in Norwich twelve years later was such a success that Bridge was at once commissioned to write a work for the next triennial festival; and both *The Sea* and the 1927 piece, *Enter Spring*, were to have a lasting influence on Benjamin Britten. When Britten extracted *Four Sea Interludes* from his opera *Peter Grimes* to make an orchestral suite, his debt became doubly clear. Bridge was dead by then, yet seems to live on at the helm. In the first Britten piece there are the threatening sounds of the North Sea clawing at the pebbles, the wail and screech of sea birds, and a forever-menacing undercurrent. The second, the Prelude to Act 2 of the opera, depicts the sun on sea and harbour, and throbs to the sound of church bells on a Sunday morning. In the third, as in Bridge's third section, there is moonlight on the water; and the fourth, just as with Bridge, plunges us into a raging storm.

The musicologist Peter J. Pirie has spoken of Bridge's 'eerie clairvoyance' and of his music's 'delicate colours, redolent of the summer sea, with a strange air of magic always present under the surface'. Certainly Bridge felt a lifelong kinship with the sea. He built himself a house at Friston where he worked, entertained friends, and went for long walks along the cliffs near Beachy Head. The house can be found along a dwindling lane beside the water tower, with a view from its front windows into a gentle cleft of the Downs above Jevington. Contemplation of that scene could have had some influence on his tone poem, *Summer*, in which the rustling of the breeze through parched grass is conveyed by an insubstantial rustling in the strings, from which a tentative theme on the oboe swells, rises, and spreads its wings over the landscape, falls, crouches below clamant horn calls, and emerges again as a quiet voice making one last appeal before sinking to rest in the ever-rustling grass. Bridge himself conducted the first performance in March 1916, when the approach of summer meant only the onslaught of more armies and the roll-call of more deaths.

For Bridge, there was darkness as well as that 'air of magic' below the surface. A pacifist in the First World War and thereafter, he was tormented by the insanity of the conflict itself and by its aftermath. To his *Lament* for strings he added the dedication: 'To Catherine aged 9, *Lusitania* 1915.' In later works a chill encroached on his spring and summer landscapes. The oboe which rose so hopefully in *Summer* has by 1927 a bleaker air to sing in *There is a Willow Grows Aslant a Brook*, as the lament for the drowned Ophelia grows bitter in mood and harsher in the scoring. Bridge adapted the atonalities and intellectual experiments of Schoenberg and Berg into an English ambience in a way which often alienated those who had hitherto admired his style, though it never shows any hint of strain or contrivance. Sometimes, also, he strayed into those forests of 'night music' we usually associate with Bartók.

Frank Bridge died on 10th January 1941 while another war was spreading destruction, and is buried in the bright, breezy churchyard at Friston. Inside the porch is a memorial door with a framed remembrance beside it.

Vaughan Williams returned to the subject of the sea in 1937 with a one-act opera, *Riders to the Sea*. J. M. Synge's portrayal of an Irishwoman's loss of her sons, one after the other, to the implacable sea is used not as a vehicle for

Frank Bridge used to enjoy taking friends along the cliffs near Beachy Head
and prawning among the rocks on the shore.

The boathouse of Padstow lifeboat, to which Malcolm Arnold dedicated a
rousing march incorporating the discord of a fog-horn.

dramatic arias and set-pieces but almost as a cauldron from which the orchestra
boils up, threatening to overwhelm the singers just as the sea is forever
threatening to engulf the entire family.

Benjamin Britten, as well as portraying the Suffolk coast so vividly, set out on
wider oceans with his opera *Billy Budd*.

Among recent composers, Grace Williams has given us a set of *Sea Sketches*;
Malcolm Arnold's Second Symphony was written for the Diamond Jubilee of
that fine south coast institution, the Bournemouth Symphony Orchestra, and he
provided an invigorating march for the Padstow lifeboat; and Elizabeth Lutyens,
a pioneer of 12-tone technique in this country, wrote *The Great Seas* in 1979.

In *The Tentacles of the Dark Nebula* David Bedford has constructed a strange
triptych embracing three stages in the life of a beach. Born in 1937, Bedford was a
pupil of Jasper Rooper, for many years Director of Music at Lancing College, and
became a keen experimenter with tonal hues, combining orthodox instruments
with electronic ones and those of modern pop musicians, allowing for spells of
improvisation in certain passages. He seems always to have been fascinated by
the heavens, producing pieces with titles such as *A Dream of the Seven Lost Stars*,
Star's End, *Some Stars above Magnitude 2.9*, and a choral work for a girls'
school, *Some Bright Stars for Queen's College*. Another contribution for girls'
choir, *The White Horse of Uffington*, shows his interest in historic and
prehistoric distances as well as galactic ones.

David Bedford's *The White Horse of Uffington*, inspired by his interest in the prehistoric, was written for a girls' school choir.

The two themes come together in *The Tentacles of the Dark Nebula*, inspired in 1969 by a reading of one of Arthur C. Clarke's science-fiction stories. In the first of three movements, a Neanderthal boy is the first human being to set foot on a remote beach. In the second, a modern boy from a nearby town plays on the beach in the company of others. Finally we peer into a future when the human race is leaving a threatened Earth for other worlds, and a child visits the abandoned beach for the last time: it waits for the end, with waves still rippling in but only for a little while. Still preoccupied with vast time scales, in 1971 Bedford produced *Star Clusters, Nebulae and Places in Devon*, in which one half of a double choir sings the names of clusters and nebulae while the other dwells on the musical syllables of Devon place names. The awesome message is that light now reaching Devon from visible stars had begun its journey when the only human life in Devon was that of Bronze Age settlements.

From the shores of Devon and Cornwall explorers have set out on many a long voyage, and many a poet or musician has in imagination voyaged westwards towards a lost Lyonesse, a Celtic dream world through whose mists ride ancient heroes and alluring damsels of immortal myth. In Thomas Hardy's poem, set to music by Gerald Finzi, the happy visitor there came back 'with magic in my eyes'.

Others continue to seek that lost land and claim it as their own. Brittany, Cornwall and Wales all pay allegiance to King Arthur. Dramatists and composers of every nation from Purcell to Albéniz have interpreted his legends to their own tastes; and how many times, be it in the tones of Richard Wagner, Frank Martin, or Edmund Rubbra in his *Ballad of Tristram* for voice and chamber orchestra, has the listener met Tristram, Iseult, and King Mark?

But perhaps our most suitable pilot across those mystical seas – or, to put it in musical terminology, the composer who can effect the smoothest modulation from this chapter to the next – is Arnold Bax, with his vision of *The Garden of Fand*, a symphonic poem about Irish sailors venturing out upon the ocean to be seduced on an enchanted island over which, at the end, the music drifts like streamers of sea mist fading in summer sunlight. His exuberant Fourth Symphony, too, is awash with the sound and romance of the sea, for Bax admitted he was romantic by temperament – 'by which I mean that my music is the expression of emotional states . . . I have no interest whatever in sound for its own sake or in any modernist 'isms or factions.'

Although at one time there were stories, which he himself did little to discourage, that Bax was of Irish origin, he was in fact born in Streatham in November 1883. In his volume of reminiscences, *Farewell, My Youth*, he confesses to regret at not having been brought up in the countryside, but he was fond of his home with its garden and little apple orchard, whose blossom in spring made it 'an island pleasance peopled with all the phantoms of adolescent dream'. Also, throughout his life he remembered a childhood evening in September on the heights of Arundel park, where the glory of a fiery sunset seemed to set the trees aflame. After another such sunset, seen from a train, he was saddened by the way the splendour smouldered into ash and, unobserved in his corner of the compartment, wept bitter tears at the ending of such a lovely day. Perhaps lingering memories of this kind were transmuted into his *Enchanted Summer* and its bleaker contrasts, *November Woods* and *Winter Legends*.

In 1910 Bax fell in love with a Ukrainian girl and chased off with her to Russia, but she proved deplorably fickle, and he suffered the humiliation of being invited to a party celebrating her betrothal to another. He returned to England – and to a growing obsession with Ireland.

Like many another English-born sentimentalist, Bax was enraptured by the legends and atmosphere of Celtic lands, and quite early on expressed his feelings in a *Celtic Song Cycle*. After living in an Irish village he admitted to having become enamoured of the memory of Cathleen ni Houlihan. He studied folk tales and fairy lore, and struggled to teach himself the Irish language, as Peter Warlock was also to do. In a symphonic poem, *Christmas Eve on the Mountains*, he tried to capture 'the sharp light of frosty stars and an ecstasy of peace' which was supposed to fall for just one night in the year upon the troubled, haunted Irish hills. Among other works in this vein are *St Patrick's Breastplate*, a setting for chorus and orchestra of an Irish Gaelic hymn, and of course *The Garden of Fand* with its ghostly evocation of the hero Cuchulain under the spell of the abandoned wife of the god of the ocean. This was written just after his marriage had broken

The first Tintagel castle was built on the site of a Celtic monastery,
derelict by the sixteenth century but living on in Arnold Bax's tone poem.

down during the First World War and he had fallen in love with the pianist
Harriet Cohen, by whom so much of his music was influenced.

Her spirit pervades a great deal of Bax's piano music and, above all, his most
popular orchestral tone poem, *Tintagel*. According to the composer himself, this
was designed to conjure up a vision of the cliff on which stood the fabled castle
where Uther Pendragon by deception lay with the wife of the king, 'and so begat
Arthur in a great hall that was next to the enclosure where this abysm is', after
which he slew the lady's husband and then married her. So much for chivalry!
Bax explains:

> In the middle section it may be imagined that with the increasing
> tumult of the sea arise memories of the historical and legendary
> associations of the place, especially those connected with King
> Arthur, King Mark and Tristan and Iseult.

The deliberate quotations from Wagner's *Tristan und Isolde* acknowledge not
merely those legendary associations but Bax's own involvement with Harriet
Cohen.

Knighted in 1937, Bax became Master of the King's Musick in 1941. On 2nd
October 1953, a few weeks before his seventieth birthday, he died suddenly while
adjudicating in Cork. Doubtless his romantic soul rejoices in the fact that his
body lies on that side of the Irish Sea where he felt intuitively he belonged, in St
Finbarr's cemetery, Cork.

8
Land of Heart's Desire

... The Isle is full of noises,
Sounds and sweet airs, that give delight and hurt not.
Sometimes a thousand twangling instruments
Will hum upon our ears.

William Shakespeare
(THE TEMPEST)

In 1895 Marjory Kennedy-Fraser, a music teacher, critic and lecturer born in Perth in 1857, came across a volume of Breton folk songs 'with apt accompaniments and singable French translations', and was struck with the idea of making similar collections and translations of original Gaelic music, for so long neglected by scholars and performers. She gave talks on Gaelic music and, growing increasingly interested in the Hebrides as the likeliest source of unspoilt material, made her first trip to the Isles in August 1905. She was to return many times, especially to Eriskay and Barra.

Though of Scottish birth, Marjory Kennedy-Fraser did not herself have the Gaelic, so the earliest lyrics she collected found their way into English via a double filter of interpretation – or, some would say, misinterpretation. Gaelic-speaking acquaintances provided her with a straightforward translation into English which the lady then versified in ladylike form, suitable for drawing-room performance and for the recitals she and her sister gave all over the country. The same sort of prettification often happened to the music itself. Although on some of her travels the collector took along a clockwork cylinder phonograph, it proved an unreliable machine, and she did not have the skill of a Bartók or Grainger in noting down vocal nuances. Odd bar lengths and rhythms which fell awkwardly on her ear were smoothed out to suit everyday pedantic tastes. In publishing her first volume of *Songs of the Hebrides*, Mrs Kennedy-Fraser justified her approach:

> We have tried merely to set them in a harmonic and rhythmic
> framework of pianoforte wrought-metal, so to speak, as one would
> set a beautiful stone, a cairngorm or the like, and have tried by such
> setting to show the tune the more clearly.

Certainly her translations of both words and music, whatever their shortcomings, were a great success with the public, but it is perhaps a pity that she published when she did, for a far more knowledgeable lady had been collecting

143

such material for years and making far better copies. This was Frances Tolmie, daughter of the factor at Dunvegan, beside Loch Dunvegan in the westerly convolutions of the Skye coastline. At the age of twenty, living with her mother and sister in her brother's manse at Bracadale, Frances was asked to do charitable work in the tiny communities scattered over bleak moors and among the lowering hills. She was to administer a knitting scheme for womenfolk of the crofts and hamlets, but, as a single young lady, must of course have an escort on her journeys. This she chose from among the older women, and as they trudged along she encouraged them to fill in the time with traditional songs and stories. In this way she had by 1908 amassed a collection of painstakingly transcribed lyrics and music which she planned to publish – only to meet Marjory Kennedy-Fraser in Edinburgh and learn that the other enthusiast's book was already on the way.

Frances Tolmie was clearly an unselfish person. She offered unstinting help and advice to anyone who consulted her on the subject, and contributed many songs to her rival's later recitals and publications. Among pieces she handed on was the well-known *Land of Heart's Desire*, in four brief bars soulfully evoking the Celtic Paradise. Later researchers with modern recording equipment have tried to capture more authentic transcriptions before Hebridean music fades away altogether into its dying sunset; but even the drawing-room versions, despite the condemnation which purists shower on their whimsies and heathery mawkishness, retain much of the feel and sound and smell of the Isles: love songs, evocations of sea and hills, snatches of praise for old heroes, and, as D.H. Lawrence put it:

> the Hebridean songs of the damned: that is, songs of those who
> inhabit a suggestive underworld which is never revealed, only
> intimated, only *felt* between the initiated ...

One dark theme which returns again and again, so that Marjory Kennedy-Fraser was able to use four separate airs in one version of it, is that of jealousy between women. *Sea Tangle* pictures a rock which shows just above water at high tide with light brown seaweed streaming to either side of it, and links the scene with the legend of a woman drowned after a jealous quarrel, her head and hair now washed by the waves.

There is a great treasury of waulking songs, often using the same dramatic themes of betrothal and betrayal, sometimes cheerfully sacrificing sense to the rhythm of work just as a sea shanty does. Well into the last century, in most parts of Britain, the common method of pounding and shrinking newly-woven cloth was by means of water-driven fulling mills. But in the remoter Scottish Highlands and Islands this process, known as waulking, was carried out by groups of women. Two teams, six a side, would face each other across a long board on which cloth would be spread, moistened with hot urine. Kneading the cloth with their hands, or with their feet when they got tired, the women would sing to ease the monotony and establish the tempo of the task: not, as one might expect, a

Dunvegan on the Isle of Skye – source of several Hebridean song
collections, home of the researcher Frances Tolmie,
and seat of the MacLeod family whose hereditary pipers were
the legendary MacCrimmons.

The dramatic landscape of *The Land of the Mountain and the Flood*, evoked
by Hamish Mac Cunn's overture.

The Snetzler organ on which Handel
is known to have played before it was
installed in the music room of Wynnstay Hall, near Ruabon, where
the blind John Parry was resident harpist.

bright and frisky chorus but usually something melancholy though steady. The length of the job was reckoned by the length of a song and the numbers used at a session: 'This one'll take three or four songs more.'

One composer greatly attracted by Mrs Kennedy-Fraser's discoveries in the Hebrides was Granville Bantock. For some years conductor of the orchestra at the Tower, New Brighton, across the river Mersey from Liverpool, he had there shown himself a champion of modern music instead of merely providing the dance music for which he had been engaged. In 1904 he followed in Elgar's footsteps by taking over the conductorship of the Worcestershire Philharmonic Society, and four years later was to occupy Elgar's old chair as Professor of Music at Birmingham University. After hearing music from the Isles he composed a *Hebridean Symphony*. He used one of the Kennedy-Fraser songs as the basis of his *Sea Sorrow* for soprano and chorus, a blend of lullaby and prayer for fishermen at sea; and to her libretto composed a sort of Celtic folk opera, *The Seal Woman*, incorporating many traditional songs, which was produced in Birmingham in September 1924.

Such attempts to revitalize music of the past were not the first Scotland had known. In the eighteenth century there had already been expressions of alarm at the decline of old traditions, and a number of well-meaning patriots meddled with old ballads and verses. Musicians jotted down fiddle tunes and arranged them for the benefit of largely English audiences. Collections such as Playford's *The English Dancing Master* include identifiable Scottish melodies which could conceivably have been carried to London when the royal household moved from Edinburgh upon James VI of Scotland becoming also James I of England.

In 1741 James Oswald, 'the Scotch Orpheus', also left Edinburgh for London to set up a music shop by St Martin's churchyard. He made a name for himself rendering old Scots airs on the cello and composed tunes of his own in similar style, many of them provided with accompaniments by Charles Burney. In this same period Allan Ramsay, an Edinburgh barber, wigmaker and poet, wrote the libretto for a national ballad opera, *The Gentle Shepherd*, and edited a collection of old Scots poems. From his *Tea-Table Miscellany* many later poets were to draw sustenance, most significantly Robert Burns, who made a major contribution to a project which had been needed for so long: the provision of lyrics, some based on old verses and some of his own writing, for melodies in the *Scots Musical Museum* and in Thomson's *Select Collection of Original Scottish Airs*. Most of Burns's work was done for no financial reward but out of sheer love for the Lallans (Lowland Scottish) speech and music of his native land. We shall always visualize 'Ye Banks and Braes o' Bonnie Doon' through his eyes, and walk with him beside 'The Banks of Allan Water', though some purists will grow angry at the substitution of a contrived but now generally accepted tune for the original native air of 'Flow Gently, Sweet Afton'.

A lot of contrivance was in fact to result from the Scottish craze which swept Britain when such collections reached the market. During his first visit to London in 1791, Haydn was introduced to William Napier, a Scottish music publisher at that time on the verge of bankruptcy. Eager for the prestige of Haydn's name,

Napier offered him £50 for a volume of settings of Scots verses with keyboard and violin accompaniment. The publication was such a success that Napier doubled the fee for another set. Few of Haydn's melodies, agreeable as they are, complement the words at all suitably – largely because the composer was not even given a translation of the words.

The same omission accounts for similar incongruities in Beethoven's settings. George Thomson, Clerk of the Board of Trustees for the Encouragement of Literature and Manufactures in Scotland, had grandiosely declared his intention to

> furnish a collection of all the fine airs of Scotland (interspersed with those of Ireland and Wales) both of the plaintive and lively kind, unmixed with trifling or inferior ones.

Scorning local artists, he commissioned international celebrities such as Pleyel, Kozeluth and Haydn to supply accompaniments and, in 1803, ventured to approach Beethoven. 'I am inclined to think,' said Beethoven, 'that a hunt for folk songs is better than a manhunt of the heroes who are so highly extolled.' In spite of this it took a lot of correspondence before he could be persuaded to contribute; not because of aesthetic doubts but because Thomson was not offering enough money. Only in 1809 was a suitable fee agreed, whereupon Beethoven set to work and within a few years had arranged some 130 Scottish, Irish and Welsh folk songs as well as producing sets of variations on folk themes which reduced later connoisseurs like Cedric Thorpe Davie to 'a mixture of laughter, tears and rage'.

Of the music of Scottish bagpipes no Englishman should venture to write. But it is worth noting that the most famous family of pipers seems to have originated in the regions from which Frances Tolmie culled so much. Hereditary pipers to the MacLeods of Dunvegan, the MacCrimmons were said to have inherited their skill from an ancestor who was given a magical chanter by a fairy. They established a sort of piping college at Boreraig on Skye, travelled in Ireland, and passed down their artistic discipline through the generations until the end of the direct line in the nineteenth century. Woe betide any pupil who dared improvise too individualistically, or stray from the rigorously established path!

At the Fourth Congress of the International Music Society in London in 1911, its presenters emphasized the contributions of different national groups in Britain, in effective contrast to the Germanic bias of earlier sessions. The French representative spoke admiringly of 'the mixture of races which gave the British their character' and pointed out that in just one programme he had found works by a Welshman (Hubert Parry), an Irishman (Charles Villiers Stanford), and a Scot (Alexander Campbell Mackenzie) – all three influential teachers as well as composers – not to mention an Anglo-Saxon 'man from the Midlands', Edward Elgar.

It was a pleasant conceit, but with a few flaws. For one thing, Sir Hubert Parry, whatever distant Welsh ancestry might have inspired his opera with Arthurian echoes, *Guinevere*, was the son of a Gloucestershire squire and was educated at

Eton and Oxford. And Stanford and Mackenzie were quick to make their way to London and establish themselves there rather than in Dublin or Edinburgh. Elgar of the Midlands was assuredly English, but wrote a more suggestively Welsh piece than ever Parry achieved: the Introduction and Allegro for strings, based on what he affectionately referred to as his 'Welsh tune', sketched after he had heard a Welsh choir singing in the distance.

To find a thoroughly Welsh Parry we have to go back to 1710, when John Parry was born at Bryn Cynan. He became the most distinguished harpist and composer and arranger for the instrument in the British Isles. Strange to note that, like Roderick Morison of Scotland and Rory O'Catháin in the seventeenth century, both of whom were known as Blind Rory, Parry was also blind. From 1734 onwards he was household musician to the first Sir Watkin Williams Wynn of Wynnstay, near Ruabon in North Wales, and continued from 1749 until his death in the service of Sir Watkin's heir. This Welsh baronet was a keen patron of the arts and numbered Handel among his friends. Handel was impressed by Parry's playing, and it may have been this contact which brought him to the notice of the Prince of Wales, later George III, who also bestowed his patronage. In 1742 John Parry published the first collection of intrinsically Welsh melodies and harp music. He composed some delightful sonatas for the instrument, and performed so impressively at a Cambridge concert in 1757 that Thomas Gray was inspired to write his poem, 'The Bard'.

Another Parry was Joseph Parry, born into poor surroundings in Merthyr Tydfil in 1841 and dying at Penarth in 1903. He struggled for a musical education but did not manage to get to the RAM until the age of twenty-seven. He produced a great many Welsh hymn tunes and songs, and threw himself into the composition of operas on Welsh and Arthurian themes unlikely ever to be seen on stage again: *Blodwen*, *Arianwen*, *The Maid of Cefn Idra*, and *King Arthur*. In 1873 Parry became the first Professor of Music in the University College of Aberystwyth and remained there until 1879. His hymn tune *Aberystwyth* is still a favourite not only in his own country but throughout the British Isles.

John Thomas, born at Bridgend in 1826, did tolerably well for himself as a conductor and in 1872 became harpist to Queen Victoria. He wrote cantatas, *Llewelyn* and *The Bride of Neath Valley*, and in 1861 was proclaimed Master of the Welsh minstrels at the National Eisteddfod in Aberdare; but his music seemed not to travel. David Vaughan Thomas, born in 1873, wrote a number of songs in the irregular Welsh metre known as *cywydd*. Obviously this wayward rhythm was too alien for other listeners and, like Thomas's work, is not heard today.

Edward German Jones, born at Whitchurch in Shropshire in 1862, eventually dropped his real surname and became a popular light opera composer as Edward German. As well as his own rollicking visions of *Merrie England* and *Tom Jones*, he completed an operetta left unfinished by Sir Arthur Sullivan, *The Emerald Isle*, and, perhaps in testimony to some ancestral Jones, composed a *Welsh Rhapsody*, whose well-worn tunes one is tempted to retitle a 'Merrie Merioneth Medley'.

As a young man Josef Holbrooke assisted his father, a pianist at the Collins and Bedford music halls, and on his behalf set comic verses to music. In 1893 he entered the RAM wishing to devote himself to composition, but had to spend much of his time teaching. He worked as conductor and pianist for a touring troupe in Scotland; and the company went broke. Nor did he find any musical stimulus from Scottish folklore while in those parts. It was Welsh legend which was eventually to exert the greatest influence on him. An orchestral poem *The Raven*, derived from Edgar Allen Poe, was performed to some acclaim at a Crystal Palace concert, followed by *Ulalume* and *The Bells*. But he committed himself with his whole heart to an ambitious trilogy, *The Cauldron of Annwn*, drawn from Cymric myth, gaining for himself a reputation as the 'Cockney Wagner'. Founded on a poetic drama by Lord Howard de Walden, the three parts covered quite a few years: *The Children of Don* was produced in London in 1912; *Dylan, Son of the Wave* in 1914; and the final opera, *Bronwen*, in Huddersfield in 1929. They are well-nigh forgotten now, but Holbrooke's free-ranging, adventurous clarinet music, probably owing much to the influence of his son-in-law, the irreplaceable Reginald Kell, will assuredly live.

In our own times some Welsh names have become respected, if not as familiar as they ought to be. Alan Hoddinott, born in Bargoed in 1929, was educated at the University College of South Wales, where he duly became head of the department of Music. A direct and even harsh composer, he argues in a distinctive tone of voice, especially in his Sinfoniettas – but is it a specifically Welsh voice other than in his set of *Welsh Dances*? In contrast William Mathias, who was to become Professor of Music at Bangor, is restrained and melodious in an amiable yet tangy way. His 1970 Harp Concerto has undoubted, if unassertive, Welsh influences, but the cast of the melodies is all his own.

In 1981 Daniel Jones's commissioned Tenth Symphony was performed in Llandaff Cathedral and named the *Festival Symphony* in honour of that year's Llandaff Festival. Earlier symphonies have belatedly been taken up by concert managers and the BBC, but do not yet threaten the dominance of the old Teutonic warhorses.

While many composers of the British renaissance turned entranced eyes towards the magical west, the most talented westerners seemed more eager to abandon their homelands and establish themselves in England. Again, this was no radical departure. John Field had left his native Dublin to work with Clementi in London, travel with him, and ultimately die in Moscow in 1837. Michael Balfe, another Dubliner, moved to Wexford in 1810 at the age of two when his father took up a post as dancing master; left for London on the father's death in 1823 to become a violinist in Drury Lane Theatre orchestra; and was then taken up by an Italian count who introduced him to both Italy and France. Balfe must have had some voice and presence, for Rossini chose him to sing the part of Figaro in Paris.

OPPOSITE
The national musical and literary contests or *eisteddfodau* held annually
in Wales for many years have been supplemented since the Second World War
by an International Eisteddfod of choral, solo and orchestral
music and folk dancing which takes place below the hills in the Vale of Llangollen.

When appointed manager of the Lyceum in London, he opened his first season with an opera he had composed himself, featuring his wife in the principal rôle. He wrote several operas, none on a native Irish theme, and made his name with *The Bohemian Girl*.

William Vincent Wallace, from Waterford, played organ and violin in Dublin for some years before being lured abroad, performing in Australia and later in the Americas until, in broken health, he retired to a castle in the Pyrenees and died there in 1865. Along the way he composed a number of operas whose titles – among them *Matilda of Hungary* and *The Desert Flower* – have little to say about Waterford or Dublin, while his greatest success, *Maritana*, was based on a French play.

On 30th September 1852 Charles Villiers Stanford was born in Dublin. In 1870 he became a choral scholar at Queen's College, Cambridge, and moved up through various posts and degrees until he became Professor of Music at the University. He was also Professor of Composition at the RCM, and it was here that his influence was most marked. Among his own works were an opera, *Shamus O'Brien*, six *Irish Rhapsodies* for orchestra, collections of Irish folk songs, and a choral ballad, *Phaudrig Crohoore*. His third symphony was called an *Irish Symphony*. Like all his compositions, these were resolutely orthodox in form and treatment, and Stanford demanded adherence to what might be called a Brahmsian orthodoxy from all his pupils. Cyril Scott was to comment on the limiting effects of his pedantry. Yet from among his pupils there emerged, after spells of subservience to this unbending traditionalist, such figures as Walford Davies, Samuel Coleridge-Taylor, Gustav Holst, Ralph Vaughan Williams, Frank Bridge, John Ireland, Arthur Bliss, and E. J. Moeran.

From Hillsborough in Ireland came Hamilton Harty, who studied under his father before becoming organist in Belfast and Dublin and then leaving for London in 1900 at the age of twenty-one. He soon made his name as a conductor, and in 1920 was appointed conductor of the Hallé Orchestra in Manchester. At his farewell concert in 1933 the programme included his own *Irish Symphony*, composed some years earlier. When a prize was inaugurated in 1902 for a work based on traditional Irish melodies, to be performed at the annual Dublin music festival, he had set to work and two years later won the prize. Initially he marked only tempo indications for the symphony's four movements, but after a couple of revisions he prepared some programme notes and bestowed a title on each movement. The first portrays the shores of a lough, the second a fair day, and the third takes us into the Antrim Hills, each section making use of cheerful little songs, sentimental little songs (on the oboe, of course!) and livelier jigs, scored with great style and humour. One wonders, though, at the foolhardiness of Harty, himself an ex-organist in both Belfast and Dublin, in putting the date of the Twelfth of July on the last movement, thus commemorating the battle of the Boyne.

The third national contributor lauded by that courteous Frenchman in 1911 was Alexander Campbell Mackenzie, who held sway at the RAM from 1888 onwards. Born in Edinburgh in 1847, he was the son of the Theatre Royal conductor and, after taking violin lessons from his father, was sent to Germany for further study. On his return he won the King's Scholarship to the RAM in 1862, worked there for three years and then went home to Edinburgh to set up as a music teacher. Although urged by Manns, who accepted some of his earliest works for performance at the Crystal Palace, to follow in the footsteps of Grieg and Glinka by 'working up national material into artistic shape', Mackenzie was cosmopolitan in temper rather than purely Celtic. Even when venturing a touch of regional colour in his first 'Scottish Rhapsody', he seemed to crave European approval by entitling it *Rhapsodie Ecossaise*. Later he used English titles for *In the Scottish Islands*, a *Highland Ballad*, and the second *Scottish Rhapsody* which he subtitled *Burns*. In 1889 this was performed in the presence of Grieg, who spoke of his own Scots origin and claimed to detect similarities between the traditional airs of Scotland and Norway.

In 1897 Paderewski gave the first performance of Mackenzie's *Scottish Concerto* at a Philharmonic Concert. In response to enthusiastic demands for an encore, the celebrated pianist said he was prepared to repeat the last movement, whereupon a stentorian critic from the gallery cried: 'Without the orchestra!'

Apart from a number of works with consciously nationalist titles, Mackenzie denied that 'the Scot keeps peering out' in his compositions. He did, however, 'mercilessly' add a bagpipe chanter to the woodwind of the orchestra in his third *Scottish Rhapsody*, subtitled *Tam o' Shanter*, which had been specially written for that patriotic 1911 Congress.

Among Mackenzie's pupils at the RAM was John McEwen of Hawick, who was to succeed his mentor as Principal of the Academy in 1924. He composed a *Solway Symphony* and a ballad rhapsody, *Grey Galloway*. Born in Greenock in the same year as McEwen, 1868, but studying under Parry at the rival RCM, Hamish MacCunn was quite defiantly Scottish in approach. His *Cior Morh* was first performed at the Crystal Palace when he was seventeen, and later he was to produce an opera, *Jeanie Deans*, from Walter Scott's *Heart of Midlothian*; three orchestral pieces, *Highland Memories*; and a number of *Scotch Dances* for piano. One of his works, the overture *Land of the Mountain and the Flood*, has survived in the repertoire because of its bright texture and stirring evocation of his homeland:

> O Caledonia! stern and wild,
> Meet nurse for a poetic child!
> Land of brown heath and shaggy wood,
> Land of the mountain and the flood . . .

MacCunn also composed a cantata around Scott's *The Lay of the Last Minstrel*, from which that quotation was taken. But in spite of his national pride he was to spend most of his life in London and die there in 1916, best remembered as conductor of the Carl Rosa Opera Company and of Edward German's light operas at the Savoy Theatre.

A later lover of Scotland and especially the Scottish border towns was Cecil

Gray, born in Edinburgh in 1895. Spending childhood holidays at Peebles, he had such happy memories of the place that he would not risk revisiting it in later years for fear of spoiling his ideal image of it. Looking back, his predominant impression was 'one of perpetual sunshine'. One thinks of Arnold Bax's similar memories; and in fact Gray and Bax were to become close friends and share other tastes, notably a taste for the mysteries and music of Ireland and the Hebrides. Another of Gray's friends was Peter Warlock, with whom in 1920 he became joint editor of *The Sackbut*, and whose biography he was in due course to write.

Like Warlock, Cecil Gray had been found unfit for military service in the First World War. And, like Warlock, he was a bit of a wanderer. Seeking a suitable atmosphere in which to compose, in the summer of 1917 he rented a house at Bosigran Castle near Gurnard's Head in Cornwall, where Ivor Gurney was later to have one of his erratic revelations. The rocks were alive with shifting hues and clothed with flowers all the way from the house to the water's edge. With skies as blue as those of the Mediterranean, everything 'combined to create the semblance of a heaven on earth, a Garden of Eden'. In winter, though, the whole region became more menacing, suffused with 'something very dire and sinister'. Altogether it sounds like the sort of atmosphere so effectively described by Algernon Blackwood and Arthur Machen. One village through which Gray had to pass regularly was so dark and chill that he felt there must be a curse on the place, an impression which Bax confirmed, sensing it as having been 'the centre in ancient times of sacrificial blood rites and unspeakable abominations, the exhalations of which still unmistakably hover around, poisoning the air'.

Other things happened to poison Gray's outlook. His nearest neighbours were D. H. Lawrence and his wife Frieda. One evening the Lawrences came to visit and sat round the fire singing German folk songs for Frieda's benefit, only to be pounced on by the police, who had been spying on them for some time in what Gray describes in his autobiography as 'a characteristically Cornish spirit of disinterested malevolence'.

With his interest in the occult, and very much under the influence of W. B. Yeats, Gray might have been expected ultimately to produce some significant work, to capture and immortalize those disturbing moods. In the end he came up with an opera about the mythical heroine *Deirdre*, in love with one of three brothers all of whom were slain by the king who claimed her as his bride. It was being considered for production at Sadler's Wells when, in 1939, another war broke out. Gray was not the only one to fall under Deirdre's spell: Arnold Bax also prepared a five-act libretto on the same subject but for some reason never got round to supplying it with music. Other composers with Celtic leanings devoted themselves more assiduously to the perennial 'matter of Britain' – King Arthur and his cohorts. And at the centre of the whole Arthurian myth, one of them began to dream of his own Bayreuth.

Rutland Boughton was born at Aylesbury in 1878. His mother, of Celtic descent, came from the Forest of Dean, near which Boughton was to settle during the closing years of his life. When he left school at fourteen, he thought of nothing but music. He got a job in a London concert agency specializing in brass bands and concert parties, and was lucky in having an employer who spotted his musical abilities, paid for him to have piano and theory lessons, and put free opera and concert tickets his way. The MP for Aylesbury, Ferdinand Rothschild, was prevailed on to pay the young man's fees at the RCM, where he studied under Stanford but had to leave early because of family financial troubles. He worked as accompanist to a popular singer of the day; tried his hand as a music critic but was dismissed for his outspokenness; struggled to have his own compositions performed; and for two years played in the Haymarket Theatre orchestra. While at the Haymarket he became involved with a girl whose drunken mother bullied him into marriage in the mistaken belief that her daughter was pregnant.

One day a young journalist submitted a sequence of four poems on Arthurian subjects which Boughton saw as 'the quarry from which to hew a huge music drama on the lines of Wagner's *Ring*'. He set to work on *Uther and Igraine* in 1908.

In 1910 he met Christina Walshe, a student who had joined the Literary and Musical Fellowship which Boughton founded in Birmingham, where he had been invited to teach and conduct by Granville Bantock. The following year he managed a separation from his wife Florence, and, with his three children, he took Christina to stay in a friend's cottage in the Surrey woods while he worked on another opera with the idea of staging it – if that is the word – by moonlight in the woods. He was unable to finish the work in time for the August 1912 deadline, but when in due course a complete version was staged it became the only outstanding success he was ever to know.

The Immortal Hour was another offshoot of the work of Marjory Kennedy-Fraser, whose songs greatly appealed to Boughton. The music itself relies mainly on the pentatonic scale of many Celtic folk songs, and the story came from the plays and poems of William Sharp under his pseudonym 'Fiona Macleod'.

Completion of the work was held up when Boughton developed another, overriding interest. At Glastonbury, he and his friends found a house called Chalice Well where they planned to establish a commune on the lines of William Morris's idealistic Socialism, of which an annual festival would be the outcome. *Uther and Igraine* changed its title to *The Birth of Arthur*, and preparations went ahead. Then word got out around Glastonbury that Boughton and Christina were not married. Local opinion was outraged. Nevertheless, by the following year the first Glastonbury Festival was staged: not in a purpose-built theatre but in the unprepossessing Assembly Rooms, and opening not with the grand performance of *The Birth of Arthur* originally envisaged, complete with full orchestra, but from necessity with a less ambitious work, the hastily completed *The Immortal Hour*, accompanied only by piano. And this first performance took place the day after the outbreak of the First World War.

Doggedly Boughton returned to Glastonbury after the war and resumed the festivals with *The Birth of Arthur* and *The Round Table*, supported by famous musicians who enjoyed the atmosphere. Local people sang in the choir and took minor roles, though ironically the very success of the annual event had its drawbacks: visitors flooded into the town, 'and when we most needed our people

for the performances they felt obliged to stay away and looked to their businesses'. Many stayed away for other reasons. They might enjoy the prosperity Boughton was bringing to the town, but they did not enjoy the fact that he was openly living in sin – not merely with Christina but now also with one of his singing pupils, who accompanied the family on a trip to Wales and there suffered a miscarriage. Christina threatened to commit suicide, but in the end settled in Glastonbury, with the children but without Boughton.

Produced at last in London, *The Immortal Hour* broke all records for an English opera. Holst and Bax praised it, and the public were in the mood for its escapist dream-world qualities. With renewed vigour Boughton worked on an opera taken from Hardy's *The Queen of Cornwall*. It is not heard today, but the *Three Hardy Songs* later extracted from it still crop up now and then. Of the more successful opera, only the *Faery Song* remains familiar to most people.

Boughton dabbled with schemes for an Irish festival, then a Welsh one, and in 1934 produced *The Lily Maid* at a week-long festival in Stroud. Meanwhile, his Communist leanings alienated many. During the Second World War he completed his Arthurian cycle with *Galahad* and *Avalon*, concluding with Arthur's vision of a red star rising full of promise in the east.

In 1960, on the day after his eighty-second birthday, Rutland Boughton left the smallholding at Kilcot on the borders of Gloucestershire and Herefordshire, where he had been living for over thirty years, and went to London for a family party. He died quietly during the following night.

In recent decades, Londoners and others from below that north-south dividing line have been readier to look beyond the borders, and regional composers are more willing to stay and work in their own part of the country.

John Tavener, born in London in 1944, wrote in 1969 what he lightly calls 'a theatre piece for children', a *Celtic Requiem* building up from one insistent chord a sombre tableau of children singing and playing games to do with love – and death. Like Bax and others before him, he has assimilated a great deal of Irish poetry and uses some of it here, together with a poem by Henry Vaughan, a well-known hymn tune, and passages from the Requiem Mass. Against a choral tapestry, a soprano rhapsodizes around a medieval Irish poem; the male soloist is amplified as a pop singer might be, and among various instrumental devices are a gong, bagpipes, and an electric guitar.

A picture of the Scottish border in summer and autumn is painted in the song cycle *Border Boyhood* by Ronald Stevenson, commissioned by Peter Pears in memory of an Edinburgh friend, Tertia Liebenthal. Here the poems of Hugh MacDiarmid hymn the pleasures of fruit-picking, days on the river and autumnal tints, and give glimpses of a footpath known as 'the curly snake' which haunted the poet's mind.

OPPOSITE
In the ruins of Glastonbury Abbey is the supposed site
of King Arthur's tomb, and at the foot of Glastonbury Tor the Chalice Well
shelters the Holy Grail – associations which brought
Rutland Boughton here to establish a festival for his cycle of Arthurian operas.

Native Scots such as Ian Hamilton and Thea Musgrave have enriched the activities of the Scottish Opera on their own ground and also built up an international reputation. A number of English-born composers have also found it rewarding to work north of the Border: a change in the tide that for centuries flowed so implacably in a southerly direction. Kenneth Leighton, born in Wakefield and trained as a cathedral chorister, has built up a reputation as a concert pianist, written major symphonies and concertos, and worked as Professor of Music at Edinburgh University. William Wordsworth has also chosen Scotland for his home. But of them all we must surely give pride of place to a musician who has chosen to settle in one of the bleakest outposts of the British Isles.

Peter Maxwell Davies was born in Salford in 1934 and went to Manchester University as a contemporary of Alexander Goehr, Harrison Birtwistle and the pianist John Ogdon. In 1959 he became Director of Music at Cirencester Grammar School where, in the words of Donald Mitchell, he 'had children composing as other teachers had them writing essays'. Rather than use the more obvious classics as they stood for school performance, he made original arrangements for the forces at his disposal and designed many of his own compositions for young folk.

In 1962 Maxwell Davies went as a visiting student to Princeton in the USA, and there worked on a subject which had been brewing for quite some while. This was an opera based on the story of John Taverner, whose treacherous services to Wolsey and Thomas Cromwell caused him to abandon music and, according to John Foxe, repent 'very much that he had made songs to popish ditties in the time of his blindness'. The moral situation was one which fired Maxwell Davies's imagination, and he worked at the opera over almost ten years, not helped by the loss of a great deal of material during a fire at his home.

Since returning from America in 1964, Davies had shared his time mainly between a Dorset cottage and work in London with the 'Fires of London' ensemble. In 1971 he began visiting the Orkney island of Hoy, restored a tumbledown croft, and finally settled there. All his subsequent works are impregnated with the island experience.

From Stone to Thorn is a setting of verses by the Orcadian poet George Mackay Brown. The *Hymn to St Magnus* is based on a twelfth-century hymn from St Magnus' Cathedral, Kirkwall. The reverberant *Stone Litany* was inspired by Viking runes scratched into the walls of the prehistoric chieftain's grave of Maes Howe, and is in fact subtitled 'Runes for a House of the Dead'. Davies's second opera was *The Martyrdom of St Magnus*, recounting the story of Earl Haakon's murder of his cousin after Magnus had refused to give battle over partition of the Orkney earldom: a story drawn from a novel by George Mackay Brown. St Magnus appears yet again in *Solstice of Light*, composed in 1979 for the Kirkwall festival, which Davies had been instrumental in founding two years earlier. It has since been performed at the Three Choirs Festival in Gloucester and has been broadcast more than once.

Solstice of Light is an uncompromising yet immediately accessible, beautifully textured work in fourteen movements for four-part chorus and solo tenor, with ornate interludes for organ – in many respects a distant relative of Janáček's *Glagolitic Mass*. The by now almost obligatory George Mackay Brown text is a chronicle of successive waves of 'incomers' to Orkney, starting with the newly created islands and their virgin hills invaded by rovers who 'rowed blindly north and north'. Green whirls of melting ice crackle through an organ solo; and then comes the vigorous race which built Maes Howe, 'earth breakers, hewers of mighty stone', commemorated in an organ solo and a chorus which, with the soloist, depict the circles of stone 'on the blank moor'. Pictish farmers and fishermen arrive; Celtic priests take over, only to be harrowed by Vikings; until St Magnus is invoked in an organ passage, and a final prayer seeks his protection against the islands' new dangers such as the discovery of oil and uranium.

This subject was taken up again in *Farewell to Stromness*, piano interludes for 'The Yellow Cake Revue' at the 1980 St Magnus Festival. 'Yellow cake' is jargon for refined uranium ore, and the cabaret-style numbers deal with the threat of uranium mining to the economy and ecology of the Orkneys.

Also in 1980 the Edinburgh Festival featured Davies's chamber opera *The Lighthouse*, in which three keepers are driven mad by claustrophobia, isolation, and their own guilty consciences, to be replaced by a fresh trio who will inevitably suffer the same fate. There is a gritty, folk-song simplicity about the voices set against a dramatic but never overwhelming orchestra of eleven instrumentalists.

Davies had also been working on a large orchestral piece which initially he referred to as *Black Angels* and then *Black Pentecost*, after one of Brown's poems lamenting the devastation of the crofting community. Gradually the music asserted itself as a symphony rather than a tone poem, and was so compelling that the Boston Symphony Orchestra commissioned a second to celebrate their centenary in 1981. Davies, though he has used stricter symphonic form than was his custom, admits that the inspiration for the work was 'one of those observations which we make which can mean a lot or mean nothing'. He had been contemplating the twitch and turmoil of wave forms around a wreck in Scapa Flow. In the tide race, tangled wave shapes had the consistency of plaited hair, twisting within themselves yet bound into an over-all pattern. In other kinds of wave the form itself altered but flecks within seemed to remain stationary. Between these polarities he found a musical equivalent, with strange intervals and disturbing blocks of sound.

The ability to stimulate the talents of young people has not deserted Peter Maxwell Davies. For the 1981 Orkney Festival he composed a new operatic piece, *Rainbow*, for Stromness Primary School pupils, and rehearsed it and gave its première in a Kirkwall school hall.

The influence of Scotland and in particular of Sir Walter Scott appears to have been more powerful abroad than within our own islands. Sir Henry Bishop did compose over a hundred pieces of musical drama for the stage, including *Waverley*, *Guy Mannering*, and *The Heart of Midlothian*, but the greatest enthusiasm came from the French and Italians. Berlioz, Bizet, Verdi and Donizetti (himself the grandson of a Scot) poured out throbbing arias on the subjects of *Macbeth*, *The Fair Maid of Perth*, and of course *Lucia di Lammermoor* – which was also used by a Danish composer, Bredal, as *Bruden fra Lammermoor*. If Donizetti had taken the trouble to visit us he might not so cheerfully have provided *Emilia di Liverpool* with a chorus of mountaineers – presumably, as Fritz Spiegl once put it, singing on the lower slopes of Knotty Ash.

Some did actually come visiting to find out for themselves; and quite a few decided not to depart again.

9
Visitors and Settlers

When music sounds, all that I was I am
Ere to this haunt of brooding dust I came.
Walter de la Mare

Instrumental virtuosi, especially Italians, discovered the possibilities of regular employment and fashionable approval in Britain long before some of the more distinguished European composers came to visit and, in some cases, to settle permanently. Barsanti and Pasquali both prospered in London and Edinburgh. Italian opera was for a large part of the eighteenth century the only form which stood any chance of success, and even German composers had to adopt its style if they were to be accepted.

In 1714 Geminiani came to England, wrote a set of *London Sonatas*, and performed them on the violin 'accompanied by Mr Handel', who was condescendingly praised for his skill. Mr Handel, too, had studied in Italy and for his first thirty years in England was to concentrate on producing a couple of Italian operas annually.

Georg Friedrich Händel had first visited England in 1710 and stayed almost a year. His favourite haunt at the time was the Queen's Arms tavern by St Paul's churchyard, where he and members of the cathedral choir met once a week to talk, drink, and sing to his keyboard accompaniment. He was back in 1712 on short leave granted by his employer, the Elector of Hanover, but, taking up with old friends and making new ones, he was reluctant to return home. In 1713 he was attached to the Earl of Burlington's household, and to celebrate the signing of the Treaty of Utrecht wrote a *Grand Jubilate* and *Te Deum* which so captivated Queen Anne that she immediately granted him a life pension. Unfortunately, after her death in 1714 the Elector of Hanover became King George I of England, and his defecting musician was in disgrace.

The popular story of Handel's return to favour tells of his writing a suite of *Water Music* to be played from a boat following the royal barge during a Thames picnic. The King and his entourage embarked from Whitehall in the afternoon and set off towards Chelsea. A band of fifty musicians in a City Company barge serenaded him all the way until he disembarked at eleven o'clock for supper 'at the pleasure house of the late Lord Ranelagh'. After supper the party returned downstream at half-past four in the morning, with the players repeating the *Water Music*. George may have taken plentifully of food

William Powell's epitaph at Little Stanmore makes an unequivocal claim
to immortality.

and wine, for he was in a mood to be pleased: he praised the music, forgave Handel, and doubled his pension.

Handel found other patrons. He stayed for a time at Canons near Edgware in the service of the Duke of Chandos, among whose household of ninety was a 16-piece orchestra and for whom Handel wrote his twelve Chandos Anthems. The house is now a girls' school, but there are some tenuous musical associations remaining in the neighbourhood. In St Lawrence's church, Little Stanmore, the organ on which Handel frequently played keeps company with the Chandos family tombs; and in the churchyard is the humbler yet by now better-known grave of William Powell, the village blacksmith. Legend has it that during a sudden thunderstorm Handel one day took shelter in the smithy and that Powell, while hammering away on his anvil, sang a catchy air around which the composer built the *Harmonious Blacksmith* variations in his E major keyboard suite. It has to be unromantically recorded that there is no mention of this agreeable tale before the early nineteenth century, and Powell's name was never even mentioned until his supposed anvil turned up and was profitably auctioned. A much earlier and likelier, although less romantic, attribution is provided by one of Handel's publishers, Lintern, who had himself been a blacksmith in his younger days and put out an edition with that title.

As rivals such as Bononcini came on the scene and competed in the field of Italian opera and song, Handel turned his attention to oratorio. In 1742 came the first performance of *Messiah*, in Dublin. Most of this, like the majority of his other works, had been written in London. Personally, however, I shall always associate *Messiah* with Gopsall Hall near Twycross in Leicestershire, now pulled down. Engaged in wartime training at the Hall, a number of us, during some wintry months when a walk to the park gates necessitated a long trudge in ankle-deep mud, were told that Handel had written part of *Messiah* while staying there; and we were of one accord that he did so because there was no other way of filling in the time in that dismal place. I have since tried to find any reference to Gopsall Park in connection with Handel, but have failed. Still I cling fondly to the belief, just as others cling to the tale of the village blacksmith.

One musical settler, also from Hanover by a roundabout route, turned his attention from music to other pursuits, for which posterity has cause to be thankful. William Herschel, an oboist with the Prussian Army during the Seven Years' War, deserted with his brother and fled to England in 1757. For a time he supported himself by teaching music, and in due course became organist at the Octagon Chapel behind Milsom Street in Bath. The town was alive with music at that time. Under Beau Nash's influence an ornate Pump Room had been built in 1706, provoking some jealous London physicians to deride the supposed healing powers of the waters, and one to announce his intention of throwing poisonous toads into the spring. Nash installed a six-piece band in the Pump Room and declared:

I will fiddle the amphibious creatures out of the hot waters; and, by

the power of harmony, charm every one on whom the toad should
spit his poison into such a dance as should drive out the venom and
turn languishment itself into gaiety.

By 1708 there was also an Assembly House to which the orchestra transferred,
and new Assembly Rooms completed in 1771 featured an even more magnificent
ballroom in which Johann Strauss and Liszt were to appear. For some years the
orchestra director was Thomas Linley, followed by William Herschel, who in
turn gave way to another immigrant – Rauzzini, the Italian castrato for whom
Mozart had written the motet *Exsultate, jubilate*, and who carried on the
concerts for some twenty years.

The reason for Herschel's retirement from the post was a change in his
interests. He left Bath and rented a room near Windsor to devote himself entirely
to the study of astronomy, where he was lucky enough to marry his widowed
landlady and acquire a substantial dowry.

Building his own telescopes, he made several discoveries, the most important
being that of the planet Uranus. George III bestowed a knighthood on him.

In our own time another foreign contributor to Bath's musical activity has
been created a KBE. After the Second World War the town became the centre of
an annual festival, at first known as the Bath Assembly. Programmes by visiting
ensembles and soloists concentrated on the music of the eighteenth century, that
period when Bath had enjoyed its greatest fashionable success. Standards were
high, and in 1955 Sir Thomas Beecham came to play his part. Unfortunately the
aesthetic achievements were not matched by financial ones, and in 1956 there was
a gap in the series while serious rethinking of basic policy took place. More varied
programmes were planned, and the director, Ian Hunter, invited Yehudi
Menuhin to work with him and take over a large part of the musical
responsibility.

Menuhin's parents were Russian-born Jews who had emigrated first to
Palestine and then to the United States, where they met and married. Their oldest
son, born on 22nd April 1916, was named Yehudi – 'the Jew' – at his mother's
insistence, to demonstrate her pride in the face of anti-Semitic feelings. The boy
became a child prodigy: as a violinist he appeared professionally in San Francisco
in 1924, went on to visit Europe, and studied under Enesco in Paris. His first visit
to England was in November 1929 for concerts and recordings. In 1932 he
recorded Elgar's Violin Concerto with the composer himself conducting, and
together they also performed it as the second half of an Albert Hall concert, the
first half consisting of Bach and Mozart concerti under the baton of Sir Thomas
Beecham.

When Menuhin took over at Bath he brought with him an orchestra which he
had assembled for London recording sessions, now to become the Bath Festival
Orchestra. He settled in England in 1959 and remained the guiding light of the
annual festival until 1969, when he and Ian Hunter turned their attention to a
Windsor Festival for four years. On giving up his duties at Bath he was made a
Freeman of the City, and the orchestra was renamed the Menuhin Festival

The Assembly Rooms, Bath, damaged by enemy bombing during the Second
World War but since restored.

Orchestra. On top of all these activities he still found time to pass on his love and
knowledge to aspiring young musicians at his own musical school.

Two years after the building of Bath's new Assembly Rooms, one of the sons of
the by-now-neglected Johann Sebastian Bach toured the south-west. Johann
Christian Bach had arrived in England in 1762 with a commission to compose
two operas for the King's Theatre, London, but stayed on to become 'the English
Bach'. For a time he shared lodgings in Meard Street, Soho, with his compatriot
Carl Friedrich Abel, a composer and viola da gamba player. Together they gave a

recital in Spring Gardens, Whitehall, and later Bach was to become a regular contributor of songs to the 'New Spring Gardens' at Vauxhall. After the success of their first venture, the Bach-Abel subscription concerts began in earnest at Carlisle House in Soho Square and then moved to Almack's Assembly Rooms in St James's. It is believed that the first public solo recital on that newly perfected instrument, the pianoforte, was given by Bach at the Thatched House tavern in St James's Street.

He became music master to the queen, wrote church music and theatre music, and poured out pieces for Vauxhall Gardens. He died on New Year's Day 1782, and was buried in the churchyard of St Pancras Old Church, now a public garden. One of Johann Christian Bach's juniors, whom he had greatly influenced two years after arriving in London, was the eight-year-old Wolfgang Amadeus Mozart.

In June 1763, Leopold Mozart had decided the time was ripe for a three-year tour of Europe with his son as the star attraction. After the young prodigy and his sister had been shown off in Brussels, the family reached London in April 1764, spending their first night at the White Bear in Piccadilly and then taking lodgings off St Martin's Lane. A few days later George III welcomed them at court, being himself an enthusiastic performer on the flute and at the keyboard. He would hardly have looked kindly on one of his subjects, Dr Samuel Johnson, who declared that music was 'a method of employing the mind, without the labour of thinking at all', and that 'no man of talent, or whose mind was capable of better things, ever would or could devote his time and attention to so idle and frivolous a pursuit'.

The Mozarts had arrived at the end of the fashionable season, but were invited to play again at Court, and made the acquaintance of J. C. Bach, who was generous with his time and musical advice and played duets with the boy. Their first public performance was on 5th June, the day after the King's birthday, when they gave a concert in the Academy of Painters. A few weeks later Wolfgang played in Ranelagh Gardens at a benefit concert for the new Lying-in Hospital, whose foundations were shortly to be laid. The family visited Tunbridge Wells, but soon returned to a more potentially profitable London.

Just when all seemed to be going well, Leopold fell ill and was advised to move to the more salubrious atmosphere of Chelsea, so it was in a house in Ebury Street that young Wolfgang wrote his first three symphonies, a set of sonatas tactfully dedicated to Queen Charlotte, and various sketches in what has come to be called 'The Chelsea Notebook'.

Returning in due course to town, the family took new lodgings in Thrift Street, Soho. Fickle public taste began to turn away from them and Leopold had to take engagements in less prestigious places such as the Swan and Hoop tavern in the City. By July 1765 he had made up his mind that there were better prospects in France and Holland. The three of them spent a few days on Sir Horace Mann's country estate near Canterbury, went to the races, and then left for the Continent.

A quarter of a century later, the manager of the London Opera wrote to Wolfgang Mozart asking him to spend six months in London and compose at

A plaque in Ebury Street, Chelsea, commemorates
Mozart's stay there.

least two operas. For some reason this invitation was not taken up, but early in
1791 Mozart was again considering a trip, this time at the instigation of Salomon,
conductor and impresario whose subscription concerts in Hanover Square
Rooms drew leading musicians from all countries. Salomon had already booked
Haydn, and suggested the younger man should follow as soon as possible.
Mozart tried to dissuade Haydn from making the journey in winter, and gloomily
forecast that they would never see each other again. He was right: he died early in
the morning of 5th December while his friend was in London achieving great
triumphs. Haydn was horrified when the news reached him:

> I only regret that before his death he could not convince the English,
> who walk in darkness in this respect, of his greatness – a subject
> about which I have been sermonizing to them every day.

During the first months of his stay at 18 Great Pulteney Street Haydn had been
impressed both by the bustle of the great city and by the widespread public
interest in music. He attended a Handel festival in Westminster Abbey and burst
into tears, crying, 'He is master of us all!' Another occasion which deeply moved
him was the annual choral festival of 4,000 children from the Charity Schools of
London, held in St Paul's. The cathedral organist had written for them a chant of
which Haydn said, 'No music ever moved me so deeply in my whole life.'

He was in demand everywhere. On the invitation of the Prince of Wales he went to visit the Duke of York at Oatlands Park, his country seat near Weybridge, and was entranced by the glorious view. In November 1791 he was a guest at the Lord Mayor's Guildhall lunch, which was followed by dancing: minuets in one room, English music in another – though Haydn noted that many tables were occupied by men who did not bother to dance but 'drank enormously the entire evening'. English social occasions have not changed much since those days!

Haydn inspected Dr Herschel's telescope at Slough; went to Ascot for the races; visited Windsor and found the view from the terrace 'divine'; and recorded his impressions of an opera at Covent Garden – 'very dark and dirty', and noisy with the shouts of various factions in boxes and galleries who argued whether certain items ought or ought not to be repeated.

On a second visit in 1794, Haydn continued as a dedicated sightseer. He inspected the fortifications at Portsmouth, though as a foreigner he was not admitted to the dockyard. Oxford conferred an honorary degree on him. In August he was in Bath, staying with Rauzzini. He visited Waverley Abbey near Farnham, and was present at the ill-fated marriage of the Prince of Wales and Caroline of Brunswick, being invited a couple of days later to direct one of his symphonies from the pianoforte. He noted that the Princess was also a quite capable performer on the instrument.

English manufacturers of the pianoforte impressed him greatly. John Broadwood was bringing out instruments with a heavier touch and heavier, richer sound and the virtuoso Clementi was turning his attention away from performance towards construction – a process speeded by Haydn's appearances in England as a substantial rival.

Muzio Clementi, born in 1752, was the son of a Rome silversmith. Before the age of fourteen he had become skilled enough at the organ to win a permanent post in his parish church. He was already composing, but it was as a harpsichordist that he attracted the attention of a rich English traveller, Peter Beckford, who virtually bought him off his father and took him to England with the promise of continuing his musical education. Beckford had inherited the estate of Stapleton Iwerne under Hambledon Hill in Dorset, and obviously fancied the idea of having a tame musician in residence.

In the event he offered little of the promised help in furthering the young man's career. Clementi had to pursue his own studies as well as he could, using such books and scores as he could lay his hands on. In that remote country house he set himself a strict routine, described in a biographical article shortly before his death:

> His sleep, his meals, his relaxation, and his studies, had each their
> appointed time and their fixed duration; and if by the demands of his
> patron on his society, or his powers of contributing to the
> amusement of the family or guests . . . the order was broken, and that
> proportion of time which he had set apart for the study of his own

Stapleton Manor, Dorset, where Clementi pursued his studies before
trying his luck in London.

profession curtailed, he drew upon the allotted hours of rest for the arrears, and would rise even in the cheerless cold of mid-winter, to read if he had light at command, or to practise on his harpsichord, if light as well as fire were unattainable.

Clementi left Beckford's service around 1773 or 1774. Plausible rumours which have survived hint that Beckford, who was later to pen violent attacks on the pretensions and morals of musicians as a race, suspected that his musically talented wife had been playing duets of more than one kind with their resident music master.

Moving to London, Clementi made little impact for a while until publication of some of his own compositions, including duets for two players at one piano, a fashion established by the young Mozarts during their stay in England. After a few forays to the Continent, he settled down as a teacher and soloist, living for a considerable period in Goodge Street, and by 1786 had been appointed 'principal composer and performer' at the Hanover Square Grand Professional Concerts.

Haydn's spells in London had an adverse effect on Clementi's audiences. The famous man being all the rage, others faded into the background. Nevertheless, Clementi was the one chosen to make formal presentation of a parting gift when Haydn left England for good in August 1795.

After that, Clementi specialized in private rather than public recitals, at the same time acquiring another reputation – for absentmindedness. On one occasion, while entertaining guests of Lord Pembroke at Wilton, he forgot to put his shirt back on after a bathe in the lake and later, growing warm while seated at the keyboard, unbuttoned his waistcoat to the alarm of the ladies present.

When the music firm of Longman and Broderip, with whom he had had a long association, went broke, Clementi decided to abandon teaching and devote himself full-time to the manufacture of new and improved pianofortes. After three years with the reorganized firm of Longman, Clementi and Company, he left to set up another partnership and brought in what was to become the famous name of Collard, with premises in Cheapside and Tottenham Court Road.

Enemies accused him of caring for nothing but personal profit, and certainly he knew how to drive a hard bargain. At Kentwell Hall near Long Melford in Suffolk was a magnificent avenue of 260 lime trees which the spendthrift owner, Richard Moore, proposed to sell off to cover his debts. Clementi bought them and cut down five or six limes to make piano keys. Then when Moore's mother, furious at the loss of the avenue, wanted to buy it back, he set such a price on it that she had to sell a farm at Lavenham to meet his demands.

There were also accusations that he had graspingly exploited the talented young Irishman, John Field. Born in Dublin in 1782, Field had been taught music by his father and grandfather and then by Giordani, who presented his boy pupil to an admiring public in the Rotunda Assembly Rooms. When the family left Dublin for London he was apprenticed to Clementi, who set him improvising at the instruments in the firm's piano warehouse to show off their capabilities. In

Clementi bought the lime avenue at Kentwell Hall, Suffolk,
as raw material for piano keys, but soon re-sold it
at a huge profit.

1802 the two of them travelled through France, Germany and Russia, where Field
made such an impression that he was encouraged to settle in St Petersburg as a
teacher and performer. He married a French girl who had been his mistress for
some time; when the marriage did not turn out too well, he took another
mistress. When he returned to London after various escapades nearly thirty years
later, his old employer had retired, first to Lincroft House in Lichfield and then to
Elm Lodge at Evesham. Clementi died on 10th March 1832 at the age of eighty.
He was buried in Westminster Abbey, and a memorial stone replaced in 1887 can
be found in the cloisters there.

John Field, however, was to receive no such honours. Resuming his European

173

travels, he took to the bottle and died in near-poverty in Moscow in January 1837, leaving behind a number of agreeable piano concertos and eighteen solo pieces on which be bestowed the name 'Nocturnes', a form to be adopted and richly developed by Chopin.

One of many distinguished visitors, Ludwig Spohr, made musical history in this country. Early in his studies he had met Clementi and Field in Russia, built up a name for himself as composer and conductor, and in 1820 was invited to London by the Philharmonic Society. We are so accustomed to seeing orchestras under the baton of a flamboyant or earnest conductor that we forget that until Spohr's time there was no such thing: the first violin or keyboard player would give such tempo guidances as might be considered necessary. At his third London concert Spohr stood up before the orchestra and conducted with a baton, to the surprise but ultimate approval of the audience. A surprise lay in wait for Spohr himself at Norwich. On a second English visit he went there for a performance of his *Calvary* in the cathedral, to find a large body of opinion opposed to the idea of a musical work, even a religious one, being presented in a house of prayer and moreover featuring professional opera singers. Nevertheless Spohr achieved a big enough success for him to be commissioned to write an English oratorio, *The Fall of Babylon*, for the next festival three years later.

Other performers and composers who set foot on these shores included Liszt, who made two journeys between 1824 and 1825 and returned in 1827, and the supposedly demonic violinist Paganini, who arrived at the Chain Pier, Brighton, in a ship named after him and strolled to the Old Ship Hotel with no baggage other than his violin. Glazunov also appeared in Brighton, some years later, for the first performance of his Third Symphony.

A visitor whose trip to London did him no good was Carl Maria von Weber. Asked by Covent Garden to compose an English opera, he took English lessons to ensure that he got it right, and, although suffering from a throat disease and unfit to travel, came to London in March 1826. He complained about high prices and declared that the only thing which cost less in England than in Germany was a haircut; conducted some of his own works at a Philharmonic concert; and produced *Oberon* in April. He struggled on as conductor of further performances but by early June was so exhausted that he decided it was time to go home. This was not to be: during the night of 4th June he died at the home of his host, Sir George Smart, and was buried in a remote corner of St Paul's until his successor as conductor of the Dresden Choral Society, Richard Wagner, put the Society's influence behind a campaign for the return of the body to Dresden.

In April 1829 the wealthy father of twenty-year-old Felix Mendelssohn decided the young man needed to travel and broaden his outlook. Friends in London arranged lodgings in Great Portland Street. For a concert in the Argyll Rooms in Regent Street he conducted his First Symphony, composed when he was fifteen, to such a rapturous reception that he gratefully dedicated it to the Philharmonic Society and soon became an honorary member.

At the end of July Mendelssohn went to Edinburgh, where he found his first experience of bagpipes excruciating. But in the ruined chapel of Holyrood where

Mary, Queen of Scots, had been crowned and where the Scottish Chapel Royal had been born, he felt the first stirrings of what was to be completed thirteen years later as the *Scottish Symphony*. He called on Sir Walter Scott, visited Loch Lomond, and marvelled at the heaths and rocks and waterfalls of the Highlands.

A year earlier he had begun to work out in his head an overture prompted by two of Goethe's poems, 'Calm Sea' and 'Prosperous Voyage'. Now he was eager to cross to the Hebrides and study another maritime subject: Fingal's Cave on the island of Staffa. On the stormy crossing several fellow passengers were ill, but Mendelssohn was delighted: while approaching the vast organ pipes of basaltic rock he heard a falling phrase which he soon sketched out and sent home to his family. This, like other ideas of his, took a few years to come to fruition as the *Hebrides* overture, nearly always referred to as *Fingal's Cave*, in which waves crash against the rocks while oboes howl on the wind and the gulls clamour.

Towards the end of this first British visit Mendelssohn spent some time in North Wales, first in a Llangollen inn whose landlord had three attractive daughters, then with a wealthy mine-owner who could boast the same number and the same prettiness of daughters. From their home at Coed Ddu near Holywell they took him on sightseeing tours of Snowdonia, and in the evenings there was always music. At one stage the girls brought him posies and asked him to 'set the flowers to music'. This led to the three fantasias of Mendelssohn's Opus 16. Roses and carnations came first, with arpeggios disseminating the scent of the flowers; the Capriccio was inspired by sprays of little yellow flowers in the hair of the youngest daughter; and third came a rippling Andante in E major entitled 'The Rivulet'.

In December the young composer went home but in 1832 gladly reappeared in London, which he praised for having the prettiest girls he had ever found. He conducted at a number of concerts and presented his *Hebrides* overture to an appreciative audience.

In 1842 the *Scottish Symphony* had its première in Leipzig, and Mendelssohn received permission to dedicate it to Queen Victoria. The feeling of old Scottish ballads, rather than their actual melody, permeates the work, and in spite of his detestation of bagpipes there are hints of their timbre in the Scherzo. That same year brought Mendelssohn back to England to conduct the symphony and other works. This time he met Prince Albert and then Queen Victoria, played before them, and made a great hit with improvisations around *Rule, Britannia!* and the Austrian national anthem. He was taken by Philharmonic Society directors by boat to Greenwich for one of the famous whitebait suppers there. He visited Manchester; and, while staying with some of his wife's relations on Denmark Hill in south-east London, whiled away an afternoon by composing a *Song Without Words* which for a time was dubbed 'Camberwell Green' after its neighbouring patch of verdure but has established itself in programmes as Mendelssohn's *Spring Song*.

When he died in Leipzig in 1847, Queen Victoria recorded in her diary the horror and distress which she and Albert felt at the loss of 'the greatest musical genius since Mozart, & the most amiable man'.

A Welsh rivulet ripples through the third of Mendelssohn's
Opus 16 fantasias.

In that same year a much more colourful personality descended upon London. Hector Berlioz had been offered a six-year engagement as conductor of Jullien's Grand English Opera at Drury Lane – some scathing references to which are to be found in the Ninth Evening of his *Evenings in the Orchestra* – and took up lodgings at 76 (now 27) Harley Street, of which his employer was landlord. Regrettably, Jullien soon went bankrupt, and Berlioz was turned out by the bailiffs, first finding other quarters at 26 Osnaburgh Street and then going home in a fury. He was back in London in 1851 as the French Government's representative on the international jury awarding prizes for musical instruments displayed at the Great Exhibition.

Like Haydn, Berlioz was overwhelmed by the annual performance of the charity schools choir in St Paul's, to which he was invited by the cathedral organist. Each school was identified by a banner in a display right round the vast amphitheatre, and Berlioz was dazzled by the dark blue of boys in the heights of some sixteen tiers, and the white of girls on the lower levels. In his memoirs he records the stunning effect of the great chord on the organ heralding the gigantic unison of

> All people that on earth do dwell
> Sing to the Lord with cheerful voice ...

The year after Berlioz's first disappointing venture to London, Frederic Chopin had arrived to find depressing sootiness in the air and an all-pervading grime. In a letter to a Parisian friend he wrote:

> As for the English women, the horses, the palaces, the carriages, the
> wealth, the splendour, the space, the trees ... it's all extraordinary,
> all uniform, all very proper, all well-washed BUT as black as a
> gentleman's bottom!

Arrangements for accommodation during his stay had been made by an ex-pupil. Jane Stirling was in fact some years older than her teacher, but had grown overpoweringly fond of him in Paris. Her unstinted praise of his genius so flattered him that he dedicated the two *Nocturnes* of Opus 55 to her. Now she and her widowed sister Katherine were using their influence to make sure he was received in the best houses in London, and, as he had completely broken with George Sand, Jane must have allowed herself some amorous hopes and fancies.

Piano manufacturers rushed to provide Chopin with instruments on which to play or compose, so that at one stage he had three grand pianos in one room. He attended concerts, played privately for Queen Victoria and Albert, and was escorted everywhere by Jane and her chaperon sister. There were some dissatisfactions however. He found it disgraceful that in England a musician was not considered an artist: that term was reserved for painters and sculptors. Furthermore, the English, he felt, had 'wooden ears' and would never create anything of any consequence in music.

Before he could grow too disenchanted, Jane lured him away on a visit to Scotland, starting at Calder House some ten miles west of Edinburgh, an old castle in which John Knox had celebrated his first communion three centuries earlier and which was now the property of her brother-in-law, Lord Torphichen. On arrival Chopin found that Jane had sent a Pleyel piano on ahead for his use. But in spite of the idyllic surroundings, with views over spacious parkland and woods to the hazy mountains, he was unable to compose. Lord Torphichen, in his seventy-eighth year, insisted on grating out old Scottish songs and telling him rambling stories about the castle ghost.

Miss Stirling, seeing the danger of boring him and therefore losing him, whisked him off to Johnstone Castle near Glasgow to stay with another widowed sister, arranged a concert for him in Glasgow, and then proceeded with a tour of other relatives and friends at Stachur near Loch Lyne, Keir House in Perthshire, and the Duke of Hamilton's palatial home. The only effect on Chopin was to alarm him. Jane's relatives lavished hospitality on him for her sake but were starting to ask awkward questions.

When challenged directly about his intentions, he made as courteous a business as he could of saying that his valued friendship with the lady should not be taken as the promise of anything more binding but, having established this, realized that he had better be on his way. In London again, he lodged at 4 St James's Place, and on 16th November 1848 had to be helped from his bed to play at a charity concert for Polish refugees in the Guildhall. This was in fact his last public performance. When he got back to Paris, the throat consumption from which he suffered grew worse, and on 18th October the following year he died.

In spite of his rejection of her, Jane Stirling paid all the funeral costs, bought up his entire effects, and had most of his furniture shipped to Calder House where she fitted out one room as a Chopin Museum. On her death the contents were left in her will to Chopin's mother and sent to Warsaw, where most of them were destroyed when the Russians moved in to suppress the 1863 Polish Revolt. But one of Jane's treasures, a lock of Chopin's hair, survived, and his heart is kept in Warsaw's Church of the Holy Cross.

In 1855 Richard Wagner was invited to conduct a season of London Philharmonic Society concerts. He spent four months in this country, under attack from the press because of the anti-Semitism in his pamphlet 'Judaism in Music', and was compared unfavourably with the idolized Mendelssohn. Wagner hated London fogs and hated the inordinate length of the concerts here. In 1870, when he began plans for a permanent theatre to enshrine his music-dramas, he was offered a site in London, but preferred Bayreuth.

Isaac Albéniz, best remembered for his *Iberia* piano suites, came from Catalonia via a European tour to seek fame in London. He produced some of his own operas and, like so many, fell under the spell of the Arthurian legends. To a libretto by Francis Money-Coutts (Lord Latymer) he began work on a trilogy, but got only as far as a half-finished first episode, *Merlin*.

Someone moving west to east also tried his hand at Arthurian themes. Edward MacDowell, born in New York in 1861 of mixed Irish and Scottish descent, studied for a time in Paris as a fellow pupil of Debussy, and then in Germany. On a London visit in 1884 he was so impressed by Henry Irving and Ellen Terry in a

Calder House near Edinburgh, where Chopin stayed with Jane Stirling's
brother-in-law and where she established a Chopin museum. The museum no
longer exists, and the house is not open to the public.

OVERLEAF
Brighton's West Pier, from which Dvořák bathed and on which Havergal
Brian's First Symphony was first performed. Stanislas Würm's
'White Viennese Band' included Gustav Holst playing trombone.

production of *Hamlet* that he wrote two pieces which developed into a symphonic poem, *Hamlet and Ophelia*. Then came another, *Lancelot and Elaine*. His *Sonata Eroica* also has a 'programme' built around Arthur and Guinevere. Another sonata, the *Keltic*, testifies to MacDowell's parallel interest in legends of Deirdre and Queen Maeve, Cuchulainn and other heroes and magicians of the Red Branch of Ulster.

Dvořák made his first London visit in 1884 to conduct his *Stabat Mater*. The following year he stayed at Brighton with his publisher, Alfred Littleton of Novello, went for a dip off the end of the West Pier, and relished the sight of

> thousands of people swarming everywhere, the beautiful English
> women bathing here (and in public), the men and children, the vast
> quantity of great and small ships, then again the music playing
> Scottish national songs, and all other kinds of things.

Ferruccio Busoni, the Italian composer and pianist, was less happy in England. He wrote to his wife from Manchester that if he stayed any longer he would need to set up as an umbrella manufacturer.

In 1898 Gabriel Fauré was invited to provide music for a production of Maeterlinck's *Pelléas et Mélisande* at the Prince of Wales Theatre, London, as well as being engaged as conductor of the theatre orchestra. Among his original pieces was a song with an English lyric for Mrs Patrick Campbell, who played Mélisande. It was not Fauré's first visit: two years previously he had given a London concert at the invitation of the financier Frank Schuster, who offered Elgar so much practical help and at whose house on the Thames, 'The Hut' by Monkey Island, both composers were to spend happy hours. Many of Fauré's songs were written while staying there.

Max Bruch from Cologne spent three years in England, most of the time as conductor of the Liverpool Philharmonic Society Orchestra. He composed a *Scottish Fantasia* for violin, harp and orchestra; and an opera, *Das Feuerkreuz*, after Walter Scott. Shakespeare, too, appealed to him, and his opera *Hermione* was based on *The Winter's Tale*.

Among curiosities which aroused comment in their day but are now forgotten was Anton Rubinstein's *Ramsgate Symphony*, otherwise called the *Ocean Symphony*. When George Bernard Shaw attended a performance at which the conductor cut out two of the six movements, he wrote that for himself he would be satisfied only when the other four had been cut.

Béla Bartók visited Wales in the spring of 1922 to stay with Peter Warlock, who during the First World War had attracted censure by trying to put on a concert of the 'enemy' Hungarian's music. There is no sign, however, of Bartók having been inspired to add any adaptations of Welsh melodies to his harvest from Hungary, Slovakia and Romania.

Paul Hindemith was in London in 1936 preparing a performance of his Viola Concerto when the death of King George V was announced. Hindemith immediately sat down in Broadcasting House with manuscript paper and a copyist, and the very next day his memorial tribute was given its first performance – the *Trauermusik* for viola and strings in four movements, the fourth being based on a Bach chorale.

A contemporary composer who has chosen a base in Britain is Gian Carlo Menotti: in 1974 he bought Yester House at Gifford in the Lammermuir Hills. Originally built for the 1st Marquess of Tweedsdale, it has a Robert Adam music salon which, when expensive restoration of the house is completed, Menotti hopes to open as a small concert hall.

Of all the immigrant musicians who at one time and another have enriched British life and the British musical landscape, one name will be most readily identified by children today. The German word 'Dolmetscher' means an interpreter, and the Dolmetsch family have undoubtedly been the most assiduous interpreters and reinterpreters of early music, as well as having transformed school music by the production of reasonably priced recorders, of which over a quarter of a million of the plastic descant model alone are sold every year.

Arnold Dolmetsch, born in France of Swiss descent, studied in Brussels and at the RCM in London. His especial interest was in old music which had been neglected through the years of lush romanticism and outsize orchestras. He began to collect old instruments, learning how to repair them where necessary and how to play them. In 1902 he went to work in an American piano factory, and between 1911 and 1914 worked in a Paris factory where he made harpsichords and clavichords. Then he set up for himself at Haslemere, on the wooded borders of Surrey and Sussex, first working at home and then establishing workshops in Grayswood Road. All the family had to manufacture their own instruments and practise daily: in due course his son Carl mastered twenty-five different ones.

The development of the modern recorder owes much to a mistake made by Carl in 1918. He left his father's treasured early eighteenth-century recorder on a Waterloo station platform, and it was not seen again until a year later when it turned up in a junk shop. In the meantime Arnold had set to work making an instrument of his own, pioneer of so many later models. The Dolmetsches and their employees were also to produce handmade viols, lutes, spinets and other instruments. Appropriate music often had to be transcribed from old manuscripts, and a whole new generation of players had to be taught from scratch. In 1925 Arnold Dolmetsch founded the Haslemere Festival of Early Music, which is still with us; in 1928 the Dolmetsch Foundation was established to promulgate his musical ideas and help in festival organization, and there is also a stimulating Dolmetsch Summer School of Early Music, held each August in Chichester.

New workshops were built in King Street in 1968. Most of the 20-odd employees came from local schools, which always had waiting lists of youngsters eager to learn this exacting craft. Supplies of material were equally dependable: seven years' supply of wood was always on hand maturing and being checked regularly for moisture content. Recorders from sopranino to the great bass were individually produced and voiced by minute trimming of plug and fingerholes, with the pitch being checked and rechecked to ensure that correction of one note did not throw others out. But the factory was best known for its plastic recorders,

The family home at Haslemere where the whole Dolmetsch enterprise began
in a shed beside the house.

moulded elsewhere from specifications supplied by the firm and assembled and checked in Haslemere.

Ten years later came a split in the firm, when Carl Dolmetsch and his daughters withdrew to continue manufacture on a smaller scale in the family home, Jesses. After a complex legal action and the collapse of the company they had left, due partly to competition from Japanese mass-produced recorders, they were able in 1982 to re-acquire the assets and expand their activities once more.

In 1981 it had been announced that the family proposed to sell more than 100 ancient instruments and some of Arnold's own creations. It was felt vital that the collection be kept intact, so a public appeal for £200,000 was made by the Horniman Museum in Forest Hill, South London, where the instruments will make an invaluable addition to musical items already displayed there.

Hammersmith Reach seen from Holst's favourite riverside walk.

10
Cockaigne

The ancient custome of this honourable and renowned Citie hath
ever been to retaine and maintaine excellent and expert musicians.

Thomas Morley

The idea for Elgar's *Cockaigne* overture of 1901 came to him one day in London's Guildhall when he was looking at memorials of the City's great past and, he said, 'seemed to hear from far away in the dim roof a theme, the echo of some noble melody'. This was typical of Elgar. On another occasion he declared: 'Music is in the air – you simply take as much of it as you want.' His own subtitle for the overture was *In London Town*, and in it he tried to convey his sense of the bustle and good humour 'and something deeper in the way of English good fellowship' which still existed in the capital. London audiences liked it from the start, and later in the year it went down equally well at the Three Choirs Festival in Gloucester.

There is still an unceasing bustle in London, but on crowded, dirty trains and Tubes and buses what remains of the good humour and fellowship? At times one fears that, along with many once cherished metropolitan landmarks, they have vanished from the scene. Orlando Gibbons was one among several who wrote pieces inspired by the 'Cries of London': what modern street cries would provide a basis for musical fantasias and variations? Mozart, set down today in old Prague, would just about be able to find his way around. How much would he recognize of the London where he once stayed?

We seek the sites of past musical activity. Towards the end of the sixteenth century, formal public concerts by the City Waits began to supersede the fragmented performances of wandering serenaders. After the Royal Exchange was finished in 1570 there were regular performances from the turret of the building, but it was not the Royal Exchange we see now: destroyed during the Great Fire, it gave way to another which was itself burnt down in 1838. The City Waits were also called on to provide appropriate music when royalty entered the City confines, and the progress of James I's queen, Anne of Denmark, from the Tower of London to Whitehall Palace in 1604 was accompanied on every side and at every corner by songs, flourishes and fanfares. The Tower still stands, but of Whitehall Palace there remains only the banqueting house rebuilt by Inigo Jones after a fire in 1619. Music booths and minstrels licensed by the Revels Office were a great feature of the annual Bartholomew Fair, and the mayoral proclamation of its opening from a door of the Hand and Shears in Smithfield was followed by a clamour of trumpets and kettledrums, consorts of fiddles, and ballad-singers. The Hand and Shears still trades in Smithfield, but there has been no Bartholomew Fair this last century and a quarter.

London innkeepers during the years of the Commonwealth had, according to John Evelyn, 'translated the organs out of the churches and set them up in taverns, chanting . . . bestial bacchanalias to the tune of those instruments which were wont to assist them in the celebration of God's praises'. After the Restoration the taverns continued to cater for those with a liking for music, rowdy or restrained, and there also grew up a fashion for charging audiences an admission fee for more ambitious concerts on the premises. John Bannister, who had been dismissed from the King's Musik after accusations of misappropriating money which it was his duty to divide among his fellow musicians, advertised in 1672 that 'over against the George Tavern in White Friars, near the back of the Temple' there would be regular Monday afternoon recitals of 'music performed by excellent masters'. Smoking and drinking, the audience heard some of the best bands in town, and Bannister himself performed on the flute. Later he produced other concerts in Covent Garden and the Strand.

Some five or six years later, Thomas Britton of Clerkenwell, whose shout of 'small coals' was familiar in the streets through which he humped sacks on his back, opened the upper storey of his coal store for recitals. Dr Pepusch, who arranged the music for *The Beggar's Opera*, was a regular harpsichordist there. Handel, too, attended frequently to play on a chamber organ and accompany Britton on the viola da gamba. These gatherings went on until the coalman's death in 1714, when many of his effects were acquired by Dr Hans Sloane.

A number of concert societies took the name of inns where they liked to meet: the Castle Concerts from the Castle tavern in Paternoster Row, the Swan Concerts from the Swan tavern, and so on. And at the Angel and Crown in Whitechapel was formed a group of dedicated interpreters of Purcell's music.

Of Henry Purcell himself it is difficult to find any physical memento in the Westminster where he worked most of his short life. He seems to have lived entirely for his music and to have left no other mark. Born in 1659, son of a Gentleman of the Chapel Royal, he became a chorister there under Pelham Humfrey. When his voice broke he was kept on as organ tuner and repairer, and at the extraordinarily early age of eighteen became Composer in Ordinary for the Violins of the Chapel Royal; five years later he became organist as well. In 1679 he took over from John Blow as organist at Westminster Abbey, writing a wide range of church music, contributing airs and dances for Court performance, and playing at the coronations of James II in 1685, and William and Mary in 1689. In 1689 he also produced his opera *Dido and Aeneas* at a girls' school in Chelsea, and shortly afterwards collaborated with Dryden on that perennial subject, *King Arthur*.

In spite of his high musical reputation, in that same year Purcell incurred the displeasure of the Chapter of Westminster Abbey. Plans for the seating of dignitaries at the coronation of William III and Mary on 11th April included the collection of fees from those requiring tickets in various parts of the Abbey, including specially built seats in the organ loft. It had been an unwritten but generally accepted custom that receipts from visitors to the loft on formal occasions were among the organist's perquisites, provided he did not lay claim to any further gratuities from the over-all allocations within the Abbey. Without Purcell knowing it – or so he later claimed – the Dean and Chapter had on this royal occasion ordained that all monies raised, including those from the organ loft, should be 'paid into the hands of the Treasurer and distributed as the Dean of the Chapter shall think fit'.

Within a week of the coronation, Purcell received a stern note ordering him to pay over all the money he had collected for places in the organ loft, in default of which his place was to be declared null and void; his stipend was in any event to be withheld by the Treasurer until further order. Purcell turned over his takings within a few days, after deducting the cost of erecting and dismantling the scaffolding for seats in the loft, and a few other expenses. It may be that he genuinely did not know of the revised rulings. It is equally possible that, having had to wait a long time after the previous coronation for his reimbursement, and having all too frequently had to wait for his salary to be properly paid, he decided to take such cash as he could and then pay back what he owed, rather than wait to be paid what was owed to *him*.

Purcell worked assiduously, as if knowing his career was doomed to be a short one. Into the year before his death he managed to cram an ode for the centenary of Trinity College, Dublin, an ode for Queen Anne's birthday called *Come ye sons of art away*, incidental music to nine plays, a number of songs and anthems, and a *Te Deum* and *Jubilate* for St Cecilia's Day. Working to the last, he died on 21st November 1695. The Chapter which had once reprimanded him for taking visitors' money published a eulogistic Resolution:

> Mr Henry Purcell, one of the most celebrated Masters of the Science
> of Musick in the kingdom and scarce inferior to any in Europe, dying
> on Thursday last; the Dean of Westminster knowing the great worth
> of the deceased, forthwith summoned a Chapter, and unanimously
> resolved that he shall be interred in the Abbey, with all the Funeral
> Solemnity they are capable to perform for him, granting his widow
> the choice of the ground to reposit his Corps free from any charge,
> who has appointed it at the foot of the Organs, and this evening he
> will be interred, the whole Chapter assisting with their vestments;
> together with all the Lovers of that Noble Science, with the united
> Choyres of that and the Chappel Royal, when the Dirge composed by
> the Deceased for her late Majesty of Ever Blessed Memory, will be
> played by Trumpets and other Musick . . .

Purcell's name is preserved in the 'Musicians' Aisle' which also commemorates Orlando Gibbons, John Blow, and Charles Burney (though Burney is actually buried in the Royal Hospital, Chelsea, where he served as organist from 1783 until his death in 1814). Also in that north choir aisle at Westminster lie the ashes of Ralph Vaughan Williams.

To celebrate the wedding of the Prince of Wales to Lady Diana Spencer
in June 1981, the set-piece for Handel's *Music for the Royal Fireworks*
was re-created in Green Park.

Handel's relics in the capital where he spent so much of his working life are not much more plentiful than those of Purcell. For almost forty years, up to his death in 1759, he lived at 25 Brook Street; but the premises are now much altered. All his later oratorios, from *Samson* onwards, were produced at Covent Garden Theatre, or the Royal Opera House, but not in the present building: the 1732 theatre was burnt out in 1808, replaced in 1809, gutted by fire again in 1856, and reconstructed by Edward Barry on its present lines between 1856 and 1858.

In spite of more than one bankruptcy and the bouts of illness which led to eventual blindness, Handel found time for a great deal of charitable work. He trained the choir at the Foundling Hospital established by Captain Thomas Coram, and in the premises of what is now the Thomas Coram Foundation, by Coram's Fields, can be found his organ keyboard, a bust by Roubiliac, and an original score of *Messiah*.

Far more extravagant than the presentation of the *Water Music* was that of Handel's *Music for the Royal Fireworks* in 1749. The whole project was so complex that a full-scale rehearsal had to be carried out at Vauxhall Gardens, on the Surrey bank of the Thames, but even this was not enough to rule out all possible hazards. On the actual day, 27th April, a huge temple over 100 feet high and 400 feet long was displayed in Green Park, erected some 500 feet from the Royal Library. The ceremonial music went off without a hitch, but when the signal was given for the fireworks to begin, the whole framework caught fire and the library narrowly escaped being engulfed in the conflagration.

Mention of Vauxhall leads us to seek in vain for a trace of the great pleasure gardens. As Thomas Hardy was plaintively to ask of Chelsea's pleasance, lost forever beneath Lots Road power station:

> Who now remembers gay Cremorne,
> And all its jaunty jills,
> And those wild whirling figures born
> Of Jullien's grand quadrilles?

The view of Lambeth riverside from the north bank of the Thames is not one to raise the spirits. Yet from the seventeenth century onwards there were thousands of pleasure-seekers bent on crossing that water daily during the season. One rhymester hymned its allure:

> Come, come, I am very
> Disposed to be merry –
> So hey! for a wherry
> I beckon and bawl!
> Tis dry, not a damp night,
> And pleasure will tramp light
> To music and lamp-light
> At shining Vauxhall.

The wherry referred to would have been one of the many craft which plied from Whitehall, Westminster and the Temple to the water-gate entrance to the gardens, where there was invariably a great congestion of people brawling, swearing, and struggling to get ashore. The smarter 'coach entrance' was at the corner of Kennington Lane.

Vauxhall's most influential developer was John Tyers, who in 1728 acquired the lease of what had originally opened in 1661 as the New Spring Gardens. Laid out with lawns and vistas calculated to charm the eye, it offered restaurants, eating alcoves, fireworks, masquerades, dancing and music of every kind, wisely providing also secluded arbours and shady walks for those more interested in dalliance than dining or dancing. Dr Arne was appointed official composer in 1745, and his apprentice Charles Burney played in the orchestra; J. C. Bach wrote songs for performance there; the youthful Mozart appeared there; one first violinist, François Barthélemon, who had settled in England in 1764, composed what is surely the most popular morning hymn tune ever written, *Awake my soul, and with the sun*; and as for Haydn, visiting on King George III's birthday in June 1792:

> Over 30,000 lamps were burning. But severe cold. There are 155 little
> dining booths in various places, each comfortably seating six

In the garden by St Pancras Old Church lies 'the English Bach',
many of whose songs were written expressly for performance in
Vauxhall Gardens.

persons. Very large alleys of trees which form a wonderful roof
above and are magnificently illuminated. Tea, coffee, and milk with
almonds all cost nothing. Entrance fee half a crown a person. The
music is fairly good.

In 1806 it was decided to abolish Saturday opening because too many disorderly
folk stayed on late into Sunday morning. Competitors abounded – Cremorne and
Ranelagh, and the Surrey Gardens, a zoo combined with musical spectacles and
flower shows – but Vauxhall flourished through much of the nineteenth century.
Sir Henry Bishop became official composer, and many songs and arias from his
forgotten operas were performed there, as well as settings of Tom Moore's
poems and one number which shows no sign of fading: *Home, Sweet Home.*

Rowlandson's famous 'Vauxhall Gardens' drawing conveys the easy-going
character of the setting, and includes the Prince of Wales and Dr Johnson and
friends among the amiably strolling populace. But by the middle of the nineteenth
century the complaints of strait-laced Victorians about increasing rowdyism and
immorality in the Dark Walk and elsewhere began to have their effect. In 1859
Vauxhall closed its gates forever.

Such of the spirit of the place as remains will be found not in London but re-
created across the North Sea in Denmark. When planning his Tivoli pleasure
gardens in Copenhagen, Carstensen visited London and adopted many of
Vauxhall's features, so that even today one can find there a number of
bandstands, alcoves and other features immediately reminiscent of the drawings
of Rowlandson and fellow artists. For quite some time, in fact, the Copenhagen
gardens were called Tivoli-Vauxhall.

As the free-and-easy pleasure grounds were being driven out of business, a
more earnest approach to the business of listening to music was evident. The
Crystal Palace, transferred from the 1851 Great Exhibition site to Sydenham in
1854, became a centre for concerts and, in due course, brass band contests. Prince
Albert had introduced many German influences into English life; others came of
their own accord, and, as in Manchester, London's most vigorous musical
promoter was to be a German immigrant.

Born near Stettin in 1825, August Manns had played the violin and cello in a
number of orchestras before himself becoming a bandmaster. He was engaged at
the Crystal Palace in 1855 as sub-conductor of the military band which provided
most of the entertainment there under the watchful eye of the Secretary of the
Crystal Palace Company, George Grove, later to distinguish himself as a
lexicographer. When the orchestra was enlarged, Manns became full conductor
and began the series of Saturday concerts which were to feature so much new
British music as well as old favourites. Later he instituted an annual Handel
Festival. His orchestra and the Hallé were to be the only permanent symphony
orchestras in England until the formation in 1895 of the Queen's Hall Orchestra
under Henry Wood.

On Saturdays, whenever he could get away, the young Elgar would walk to
Worcester station to catch an early train and dash across London to the Crystal

Palace in the hope of hearing at any rate part of the rehearsal. He would attend the actual afternoon concert and then race back to Paddington for the train home. When he was twenty-six his own *Sevillana* had its first London performance at a Crystal Palace concert, and many other of his works were to be heard there, including the brass band test piece, the *Severn Suite*.

Shortly before the First World War, Vaughan Williams discussed with his friend George Butterworth the progress of an orchestral tone poem about London. It was Butterworth who persuaded him that the work ought to be reshaped as a four-movement symphony and who helped with the copying and with preparation of programme notes for the first performance in March 1914. The *London Symphony*, dedicated to Butterworth, was revised by the composer and re-presented in 1920. It begins with a characteristic Vaughan Williams folk-song phrase, an aspiring fourth freeing itself from the lower strings and struggling to breathe a tune. Everything is very busy, with hints of urchins whistling cocky little tunes, street cries, the chimes of Big Ben, a cabby's shout, a mouth-organ, and the cry of a lavender seller. The slow movement has been said to represent one of London's more gracious squares. The composer marked the third as a Nocturne, but still there is a fret of activity through what one might see as a London evening haze, with one steadying tune emerging like someone humming a street ballad. The last movement marches us on into a swirling Allegro, and ends quietly resonant with the chimes of Big Ben once more.

During his years of work at the RCM and as church organist, between creative interludes in the Channel Islands and before finally settling in Sussex, John Ireland lived in a Chelsea studio. His surroundings, though not as dear to him as the Downs and prehistoric megaliths, provoked many a pictorial composition. The *Three London Pieces* all come from personal observation. The first is a Barcarolle suggesting the slow tide of *Chelsea Reach*. The second, *Ragamuffin*, was hastily sketched out on the vestry piano at St Luke's Chelsea, when Ireland arrived there for choir practice after hearing a grubby little lad whistling down the street. In the third piece, *Soho Forenoons*, we hear the street buskers and gossiping shopkeepers of a Soho which bears little resemblance to the porn-shop and grubby cinema sordidness of today.

After his *Downland Suite*, Ireland conceived another work for brass band which he first dubbed *A Comedy Overture* but then converted into a *London Overture* for full orchestra. After a slow, declamatory introduction we are taken into a lolloping Allegro whose main theme was suggested by a bus conductor's cry of "dilly . . . Piccadilly'. After a meditative passage, which retains some of the brass sonority of the original, the Piccadilly motif returns jauntily and carries us to our destination.

Another local piece was the *Ballade of London Nights*, a large-scale piece for piano which Ireland decided he didn't like. It was withheld until after his death, and then edited for publication by Alan Rowlands. One cannot understand what Ireland's objections were: it is a compelling, intense work – but perhaps the intensity derives from some personal pain which in the end he did not wish to exhibit to the world.

The Gluepot bar at the George, behind Langham Place, earned its name from
the difficulty experienced in dragging orchestral players out of it in
time for a concert at Queen's Hall.

During the Second World War he was commissioned by the BBC to write an
Epic March which, in spite of his hatred of the war itself, became a tribute to the
heroism of ordinary people during the Blitz.

While those air raids on London were gathering momentum, Arnold Bax's *A
London Pageant* was given at what was to be the last Henry Wood Promenade
Concert in Queen's Hall, on 7th September 1940. The season was only halfway
through, but the Nazi attacks were becoming so savage that it was decided to
abandon the concerts. Twice thereafter the hall was seriously mutilated by blast,
but was repaired well enough for Malcolm Sargent to conduct a performance of
Elgar's *The Dream of Gerontius*. That same night of Saturday 10th May 1941, one
of the fiercest of all air raids on London hit City churches and company halls, the
chamber of the House of Commons, and Queen's Hall, which was burnt out and
never rebuilt. On its site near All Souls' church, Langham Place, now stands a
modern hotel.

Towards the end of the First World War, when Zeppelins were regarded as the
ultimate in terror bombing, a unique concert had been organized in Queen's Hall
on behalf of Gustav Holst. Holst's early career as a trombonist took him from

Brighton's West Pier to other seaside entertainments, the Carl Rosa Opera on tour, and to London during the pantomime season, when he earned enough to rent a bed-sitter near Hammersmith Broadway. This district was to be his base during most of his London years. He was made conductor of the Hammersmith Socialist Choir and there met Isobel Harrison, who became his wife and moved with him into two furnished rooms over a shop in Shepherd's Bush. He got a teaching job in a girls' school at Dulwich, then was appointed musical director at St Paul's Girls' School in Brook Green, Hammersmith, a post which he retained until his death. In 1907 he was also appointed musical director of Morley College, next to what was then the Old Vic in Waterloo Road. The Holsts could by then afford to rent a small Regency house by the river at Barnes, where the composer had his own music room at the top of the house. The front now bears a memorial plaque. He also had a sound-proofed study at St Paul's school, where he wrote his *St Paul's Suite* for strings for the girls in the orchestra, and ultimately completed *The Planets*.

The schoolgirls rallied round in 1918 for the first performance of *The Planets*. Holst was due to leave for Istanbul as YMCA organizer of musical education among the troops awaiting demob, and the always beneficent Balfour Gardiner decided that before departing he should hear the work properly played. Gardiner hired Queen's Hall, engaged the nineteen-year-old Adrian Boult to take the orchestra sight-reading through the score, and whipped up an audience of well-wishers and anyone else who could be persuaded to fill up the vacant seats. Sir Adrian Boult later observed that every girl in St Paul's must have been dragged in to copy the parts, and Imogen Holst refers to musically-minded German prisoners of war who volunteered to cooperate.

When Holst was back from overseas and ensconced once more in his Brook Green study, young Arthur Bliss came to show him the scores of two orchestral studies, and was forever impressed by Holst's 'utter honesty of opinion that riveted attention'.

Hammersmith seems never to have lost its appeal. Holst used to enjoy meeting friends in The George on the Broadway – a pub whose wide frontage bulges with upper-storey windows in an architectural mish-mash which nevertheless fits very well into the turmoil of that busy junction. A favourite walk of Holst's is perhaps not as pleasurable now as it was in his day, but it still offers much to the leisurely stroller. It begins along the riverside path from Hammersmith bridge and finishes in the grounds of Chiswick House. The vista plays a large part in his Prelude and Scherzo, *Hammersmith*, commissioned by the BBC Military Band but later rescored for full orchestra. Holst declared his intention of expressing his feelings for the district not in any programmatic way but by somehow capturing the essence of crowds of local people and the calmer background of the river, 'that was there before the crowd and will be there presumably long after, and which goes on its way largely unnoticed and apparently quite unconcerned'.

Perhaps as he sauntered along Lower Mall he, too, was happy to be unnoticed and unconcerned – or concerned only with the music he was hearing in his head. Past a fantasy of balconies and grilles, diminutive gardens and the wide doors of

Prehistoric monsters made of plaster are all
that remain of the Great Exhibition of 1851 on the
Sydenham site of the Crystal Palace, home
until 1936 of orchestral, brass band and choral concerts.

The Lammermuir hills, whence came *Lucia di Lammermoor, Fidanzata*
Fiancée de Lammermoor, interpreted from Sir Wal

mermoor, Bruden fra Lammermoor, The Bride of Lammermoor, and
by operatic composers into many languages.

Sir Arthur Sullivan watches over Victoria Embankment Gardens near the
Savoy Theatre in which his popular collaborations with W.S. Gilbert
distracted attention from his attempts at more serious music.
Their theatrical manager Richard d'Oyly Carte is commemorated by a
window in the Queen's Chapel of the Savoy, and a nearby public house
named after them contains souvenirs of the partnership.

rowing clubs he would follow the slow curve of the Thames, some part of it forever catching and playing with the light at any hour of the day. Upper Mall takes one past The Dove (or Doves), where James Thomson is said to have written the poem on which Haydn based *The Seasons*, and past the bland Georgian façade of Kelmscott House, where William Morris established his printing press and where, in his early days in London, Holst had attended Sunday lectures by George Bernard Shaw and Morris himself.

Looking back through the span of Hammersmith bridge today, Holst would scarcely recognize the chunky skyline of high-rise flats and offices. On along Chiswick Mall and the path beside the church into Powell's Walk, and we cross the road into the grounds of Chiswick House, built by that Lord Burlington who had been Handel's first patron in England. Traffic on that road is far fiercer than it would have been then, and once Holst was in the grounds, what would he have made of the thundering descent of jets above the great glasshouse on their way into Heathrow: would he have found some way of incorporating the traffic's insistent rumble and the continued roar of aircraft into his music?

During his last illness in late 1933 and early 1934 he was still writing of or for Hammersmith, in his *Brook Green Suite* for the St Paul's string orchestra.

If we half-close our eyes and listen, perhaps the music can evoke for us what he saw. And if we choose the right accompaniment, there are earlier, enticing visions to be glimpsed across the years: the lights of Vauxhall, the carriages arriving in Soho Square for a Bach-Abel recital, the innovation of Promenade Concerts under Musard in Drury Lane and Jullien at Covent Garden. Further back still are the voices of young singers at Temple Bar on state occasions, and the jubilation of City trumpeters and Waits accompanying a new Mayor to his barge. Tallis walked here; Orlando Gibbons heard these street cries; Purcell sat at this organ.

Of all musical events, one of the most symbolic in the history of the capital was the defiant series of lunchtime concerts given in the National Gallery during the Second World War. Most of the valuable pictures had been removed, and their place was taken by pianists, singers, and chamber groups. Finzi's *Five Bagatelles* for clarinet and piano were first heard here. Troops on leave and people working in the neighbourhood snatched a sandwich lunch while listening to Myra Hess, deservedly created a Dame of the British Empire for her part in establishing the recitals. Even the sound of German was not banned: Elisabeth Schumann, loveliest of *lieder* interpreters, trembled at the prospect of the reception she might expect there at such a time – and was almost in tears at her rapturous welcome.

With our eyes open again, but the echoes still not hushed, perhaps we may most appropriately play ourselves out in resounding fashion with Handel's setting of Dryden's *Ode on St Cecilia's Day*:

> So when the last and dreadful Hour
> This crumbling pageant shall devour,
> The Trumpet shall be heard on high,
> The dead shall live, the living die,
> And Music shall untune the sky!

St Cecilia serenely bestows her patronage on the Royal College of Organists
near the Albert Hall, London.

Bibliography

Among the books which, in addition to providing confirmatory references and essential basic information, have in themselves been a pleasure to read are the following:

Bassin, Ethel, *The Old Songs of Skye: Frances Tolmie and her Circle* (Routledge & Kegan Paul, 1977)

Bax, Arnold, *Farewell, my Youth* (Longmans Green, 1943)

Bent, Margaret, *Dunstaple* (Oxford, 1981)

Berlioz, Hector (transl. C. R. Fortescue), *Evenings in the Orchestra* (Penguin, 1963)

—— (transl. David Cairns), *Memoirs* (Gollancz, 1969)

Bliss, Arthur, *As I Remember* (Faber, 1970)

Blunt, Wilfrid, *On Wings of Song – a Biography of Felix Mendelssohn* (Hamish Hamilton, 1974)

Brown, David, *Thomas Weelkes* (Faber, 1969)

Copper, Bob, *A Song For Every Season* (Heinemann, 1971)

Cox, David, *The Henry Wood Proms* (BBC, 1980)

Davie, Cedric Thorpe, *Scotland's Music* (Blackwood, 1980)

Delius, Clare, *Frederick Delius* (Nicholson & Watson, 1935)

Dibdin, Charles, *Professional Life and Songs* (Dibdin, 1803)

Eastaugh, Kenneth, *Havergal Brian* (Harrap, 1976)

Farmer, Henry, *History of Music in Scotland* (Hinrichsen, 1947)

Fellowes, E. H., *English Madrigal Composers* (Oxford, 1921)

Flood, Grattan, *A History of Irish Music* (Browne & Nolan, 1905)

Foreman, Lewis (ed), *British Music Now* (Elek, 1975)

Graves, C. L., *Hubert Parry* (Macmillan, 1926)

Gray, Cecil, *Musical Chairs* (Home & van Thal, 1948)

—— *Peter Warlock* (Cape, 1934)

Hogwood, Christopher, *Music at Court* (Gollancz, 1980)

Holst, Imogen, *Britten* (Faber, 1966)

—— *Holst* (Faber, 1972)

Hurd, Michael, *Immortal Hour – the Life and Period of Rutland Boughton* (Routledge, 1962)

—— *The Ordeal of Ivor Gurney* (Oxford, 1978)

Jefferson, Alan, *Delius* (Dent, 1972)

Jordan, Ruth, *Nocturne – a Life of Chopin* (Constable, 1978)

Johnson, David, *Music and Society in Lowland Scotland in the Eighteenth Century* (Oxford, 1972)

Landon, H. C. Robbins, *Collected Correspondence and London Notebooks of Joseph Haydn* (Barrie & Rockliff, 1959)

Longmire, John, *John Ireland* (John Baker, 1969)

Lonsdale, Roger, *Dr Charles Burney* (Oxford, 1965)

MacCormick, Donald, *Hebridean Folk Songs* (Oxford, 1969)

Mackenzie, Alexander Campbell, *A Musician's Narrative* (Cassell, 1927)

Mackerness, E. D., *Social History of English Music* (Routledge, 1964)

Matthews, David, *Michael Tippett* (Faber, 1980)

McVeagh, Diana M., *Edward Elgar* (Dent, 1955)

Menuhin, Yehudi, *Unfinished Journey* (Macdonald & Jane's, 1977)

Orrey, Leslie, *Programme Music* (Davis-Poynter, 1975)

Osborn, James (ed), *Autobiography of Thomas Whythorne* (Oxford, 1955)

Palmer, Christopher, *Herbert Howells* (Novello, 1978)

Palmer, Roy, *A Ballad History of England* (Batsford, 1979)

Piggott, Patrick, *The Life and Music of John Field* (Faber, 1973)

Pirie, Peter J., *The English Musical Renaissance* (Gollancz, 1979)

Plantinga, Leon, *Clementi, his Life and Music* (Oxford, 1977)

Schenk, Erich (transl. R. & C. Winston), *Mozart and his Times* (Secker & Warburg, 1960)

Warlock, Peter, *Frederick Delius* (Bodley Head, 1923; revised 1952)

Warwick, Alan R., *A Noise of Music* (Queen Anne Press, 1968)

Westrup, A. J., *Purcell* (Dent, 1975)

Woodfill, Walter, *Musicians in English Society* (Princeton, 1953)

Woods, Fred, *Folk Song in Britain* (Warne, 1980)

Young, Percy M., *Debussy* (Benn, 1968)

Zimmerman, Franklin B., *Henry Purcell, 1659–1695* (Macmillan, 1967)

Acknowledgements

Most of this book arose from the inspiration of the scenes themselves and the music which led me to those scenes. Innumerable snippets of information from brochures, newspaper reports, music magazines, radio programmes and the reminiscences of friends and other people met on my travels, pointed the way to places I might otherwise have missed. In particular I must thank D. H. Webb of Malvern; Gavin Henderson of South Hill Park Arts Centre, Bracknell, who was both entertaining and instructive; W. G. Heaton of the Arnold Dolmetsch company; J. P. M. Phillips of Kentwell Hall; Humphrey Phelps of Westbury-on-Severn for assistance with the stories of Herbert Howells and Ivor Gurney; the library staff of Newcastle upon Tyne; and the staff of the National Library of Scotland, Edinburgh, who cheerfully went to a lot of trouble at very short notice.

The debt I owe to Ian Pleeth not just for his photographs but for the helpful suggestions and comments made on his travels, and for his patience and good humour throughout, is incalculable.

Index

Italicized figures indicate an illustration page